Sacred Choices

*Diary of a Medical Intuitive: One Woman's Eye-Opening
Journey from No-Nonsense ER Nurse to
Open-Hearted Healer and Visionary*

*Guidance 24/7: How to Open Your Heart
and Let Angels into Your Life*

Sacred Choices

THINKING OUTSIDE
THE TRIBE
TO HEAL YOUR SPIRIT

Christel Nani

HARMONY BOOKS
NEW YORK

Published in the United States by Harmony Books,
an imprint of the Crown Publishing Group,
a division of Random House, Inc., New York.
www.crownpublishing.com

Harmony Books is a registered trademark and the Harmony
Books colophon is a trademark of Random House, Inc.

Library of Congress Cataloging-in-Publication Data
Nani, Christel.
Sacred choices : thinking outside the tribe to heal your spirit /
Christel Nani.—1st ed.
p.   cm.
1. Self-actualization (Psychology).   2. Self-talk.   3. Belief and
doubt.   I. Title.
BF637.S4N363   2006
158—dc22   2006013047

ISBN-13: 978-0-307-34165-5
ISBN-10: 0-307-34165-8

Printed in the United States of America

Design by Jennifer Ann Daddio

10 9 8 7 6 5 4 3 2 1

First Edition

To Dr. Rebecca Grace, my best friend.
Thank you for your unwavering encouragement and support.
Your brilliant contributions, editorial insights, and laughter
continue to make my journey fun and easy. You are the best!

Contents

Foreword

This is the book I wish I'd had when Christel was working with me to heal my MS. Maybe you have been given a diagnosis, maybe you know you're sick but your doctor can't pin it down yet, or maybe you suffer from a spiritual malady, feeling stuck, lost, knowing there's something more, but you don't know how to get there. You may very well find your answer in these pages.

This book is by the best spiritual teacher I know. Her teachings are practical, real, and effective. As you read, you will have many choices to make. That's the essence of Christel's teachings: making people aware of what their choices have been and how they can now choose differently. I hope your first choice is to believe that healing can be much simpler than you might think, quicker than you've been taught, and much more fun than you've suspected. And this book can show you how. As they say in AA, all you have to do is give up all your old ideas.

As a psychologist, when I got sick I knew of the mind-body connection, that one's thoughts and attitudes could have a major impact on how one dealt with illness and maybe even contribute to a positive or negative outcome. From my metaphysical studies, I had been taught that certain thoughts could produce certain illnesses. But no one told me which thoughts were causing my nervous system to rigidify with scars instead of soft conductive myelin. Did I have anti-neuron thoughts? Did I hate my spinal cord and brain? Which of my thoughts were encouraging my limbs to lose feeling and coordination?

I searched through books, but not one gave an indication of which of my thoughts might be responsible for the rapid deterioration of my health. I thought I was doing everything right and I was confused and scared; I knew there had to be a connection, but what was it?

When I started working with Christel, she gently introduced me to the idea of tribal beliefs—powerful, unconscious ideas that guide our behavior and choices and can affect our health. I was intrigued; at last someone could tell me the thoughts that had made me sick. "This will be easy," I thought. "I can change them, and presto, I'll be well again."

What I wasn't prepared for was that the things inside me that helped make me ill were precious to me, ideas and values that I had learned from my parents, two people I adored and loved deeply. And they had learned those ideas from my grandparents, people whom I also loved and respected. I wanted them all to be so proud of me.

I just could not believe that my values, those things that defined me, made me a good person and helped me feel good about myself, were somehow wrong. It just did not make sense. Everyone knows that working hard is important; that nothing comes free; that you have to earn your good; that unless you're working hard, you're a drain on society; and, of course, that marriage is forever. I remember once that one of my therapy supervisors had cautioned me never to mess with a person's values in therapy. They were sacrosanct, to be respected and honored, but never questioned or changed.

And here was this Medical Intuitive, questioning my values! Or at least that's what I thought she was doing. And so I resisted, not seeing any connection between these wonderful and inspiring ideals that I strived to live by and my difficulty walking, holding on to silverware, and feeling my feet and legs. I was proud of who I was, a hardworking, productive member of society, making a success of myself in my own business, watching out for my dad after my mom's death, and participating in a perfectly happy marriage.

The only problem is that once Christel "Reads" your soul, you cannot ignore what she tells you or make it go away, no matter how upset you are by what you hear. It simply demands your attention and you cannot avoid it. Christel is like a megaphone for your soul, helping you hear what you have been shutting out; and once you hear, you are forever changed.

So even though I was angry and spent a few months fighting her (it really is a wonder she didn't fire me, I was a terrible client!), I slowly started to change. (Did I mention that rigidity of thinking is one of the energetic predispositions to MS?) But the point is, I did change, and believe me, if a psychologist can change, then you certainly can. My body healed completely, and my spirit talks to me daily (and I listen!).

This book can help you heal. It can help you be happier,

more creative, more in the flow. It can even help you connect with God. There's nothing worse than a tribal telling us we don't deserve God's love to interfere with the flow of blessings into our lives.

You will, however, have to question some of your most deeply held beliefs, ideas, and, yes, even some of those important and precious values. In exchange, you will hear the voice of your spirit, the soft guidance of your intuition, and you will know what it's like to have a pure energetic intention, the kind that manifests easily.

You might have to change your way of thinking, and maybe act differently than you think those you love want you to act. It is a decision we all must make at some point—to listen to our bodies and our spirit, to let go and trust that, even though it seems to violate everything we've been taught, our spirit will never lead us in any direction that isn't magnificent.

My father died before my body completely healed, but he saw the lightness of my heart increasing daily. He told me how this filled him with deep happiness. This hardworking, dedicated Kraut (a term of endearment used in our family to describe our German heritage) preferred to see me happy rather than working myself into a wheelchair.

So, yes, you have to change if your tribals are making you ill and you don't want to be sick anymore. The end result is your healing, and you never know, maybe even the admiration and respect of your tribe. It's great to be an inspiration; we need every bit we can get on this planet.

Christel Nani is an amazing, beautiful human being. Her dedication to helping people find God through healing their blocks is awesome. So is her dedication to eating Dove dark chocolate and having a great time in life. She lives what she teaches, she's connected to God, she's real, and she'll never waste your time teaching spiritual platitudes. She gets to the heart of the matter quickly, and it's this authenticity that draws people to her.

Now go read; change whatever is crimping your spirit, and get on with the life God intended for you!

—Rebecca Grace, Psy.D.

Sacred Choices

I.

What Happened to My Passion?

IS YOUR LIFE AS YOU

WANT IT TO BE?

Have you ever wondered why you work so hard, grief is so hard to overcome, or just when things start to go well, something bad happens? I may have the answer.

Your ancestors taught you how to work, how to grieve, and why bad things happen. You have taken for granted that in their desire to protect you, they prepared you adequately for life by teaching you the way of the tribe—what they valued and what they believed to be true. These tribal beliefs are the inherited ideas about the way life works, passed down to you from anyone who had power or authority over you as a child—pretty much anyone who was taller than you were. Some of these beliefs cause you to make choices that make your life harder than it needs to be, creating conflicts and inner turmoil often marked by repetitive themes and patterns. For example:

- When you are making a decision, do you feel torn between what you are supposed to do and what you would like to do?
- Do you have dreams that excite you, but find yourself exhaling in defeat as your thoughts proclaim, "That's not realistic—I can't do that"?
- Does it trouble you that some of the things you do conflict with your intuition or inner knowing?
- In general, do you feel stuck or frustrated with the way things are?

These are not unsolvable conundrums. They are the result of limiting tribal beliefs. A limiting tribal belief is any tribal belief that holds you back from your best life. The good news is that they can quickly and easily be changed once you know the steps to follow. In this book, I'll walk you through those steps so that you can experience the health and happiness of a life in tune with who you really are and what you really want.

At first, you aren't even aware that you are making choices at all. You are simply following the tribal way, even when you believe you are thinking for yourself and doing what is best for you. Consider the student who pursues a college degree in an area that offers a safe career path but does not excite her, or the man who gets married despite his doubts because everyone tells him how lucky he is to have found someone so nice. Or perhaps you are justifying staying in a career you no longer enjoy because the pay is good, or a draining relationship because you've been together for a long time. These are all examples of lives driven by limiting beliefs, not the heart's desire. Unfortunately and paradoxically, some tribal rules are contrary to your authentic nature and needs. Even a life that looks successful on the outside can leave you wondering if this is as good as it gets, because you recognize on a deep level that something is missing. And it is.

A limiting belief confines your exceptionality.

What's missing is a deep satisfaction with your life, alignment with your soul, happiness that wells up and overflows, peace of mind, and a general sense of well-being. One reason you are left wanting is that tribal beliefs can make you think you want things that you really don't, and when you get them you wonder why you aren't wowed by them. This is but one symptom of a person at odds with his spirit and not living an authentic life. And a life without authenticity quickly becomes a life without passion.

Remember, most often you are not conscious of these limiting beliefs. I can help with this. If you were standing before me right now, I could "Read" what's happening inside you as easily as you can read the front page of your local paper. As a

Medical Intuitive, what I actually Read is what's called your *energetic blueprint.* It contains information about your beliefs, your perceptions about yourself and others, your connection with God or a Higher Power, and how high or low your energetic level is. It is a map that shows where you are putting your energy and whether those places are life-enhancing—or not.

Your energetic blueprint is very detailed. It allows me to see exactly:

- Where you are stuck or unhappy.
- How trapped you feel.
- What contributed to your illness—or why you are about to become ill.
- Why you aren't getting what you say you want.
- The conflicts between your limiting beliefs and your spirit.
- Who you are meant to be and what's keeping you from being that person.

In short, your energetic blueprint shows me the conflict between who you have become—which is what others expect and want you to do and what you think you should do, and who you really are—*the authentic you, replete with your gifts, talents, and purpose being guided by your soul or spirit.*

I understand and have overcome this conflict. I knew two things at the age of eight: that I would be an emergency room nurse, and that I have a gift to Read people's energy. In the many years since, there have been times when I ignored my gift and times when I cursed it. As you can imagine, there are many limiting beliefs about such a gift that could have altered the course of my life away from listening to my spirit. I had to choose what was truth for me—what beliefs resonated with my spirit, raised my vibration, and allowed me to be authentic and fulfill my purpose in life. I honed my gifts working as an RN in Emergency/Trauma for more than sixteen years. During that time, my abilities served me well and saved lives. Had I neglected my spirit and become complacent or refused to further examine and uncover my limiting beliefs, I would have stayed in the ER. However, spiritual evolution demands movement on our part.

My choice to leave my beloved ER and devote myself full-time as a Medical Intuitive was originally not my choice at all. Rather, it was the most seemingly illogical guidance (leave the exciting job that I was passionate for—one I had traversed the ladder of success to get—for a completely unknown future) I had ever received. I have since learned that guidance often does fly in the face of logic, but that if you follow it, you will uncover your purpose(s) in life.

A limiting belief will severely hamper your ability to follow your guidance or inner knowing.

Since I always knew I was meant to be an ER nurse, I never imagined there would be another purpose for me—I felt so blessed in my profession; my clairvoyant gifts and abilities made it easy for me to help people in crisis—not just their bodies, but their hearts and minds, too. It was my unwanted—I'd like to ignore it—guidance that revealed my next purpose in this life: to continue helping people in crisis, not just physical or emotional crises but also crises of spirit.

While ER/Trauma nursing will always be an exciting part of my blueprint, I am just as passionate about helping people learn to hear the voice of their spirit and discover their purpose. For this reason, I became an interfaith minister—to talk to people about God or a Higher Power in a way that is meaningful for them. I help people to identify their gifts and talents so that they can be of service to others and come closer to actualizing their purpose in life. *Sacred Choices* will help you identify limiting tribal beliefs that will conflict and derail you from that path.

It happened to Anna. She worked hard for her college degree and to become a professional, self-reliant woman. Her family and friends applauded her success, yet she remained non-plussed by her achievements. She had done everything right (according to her tribal beliefs), but now, in her midthirties, she was unhappy and restless, and I saw exactly why. I asked her why she was pursuing her career when she didn't really want to. It took her a year and a half to answer me.

It was only after Anna whispered to me what she truly wanted that the tears began to flow. She was horrified by her confession. All she had ever wanted was to be a stay-at-home mom. And she didn't want one child but a brood of them, enough for a basketball team. I had seen her desire in her blueprint, and the tribal belief that criticized that desire. Her family had taught her that stay-at-home moms were lazy, weak, and stupid because all they wanted from life was to raise children and be taken care of by a man. Because Anna feared the judgment of her family and peers, she had ignored her heart. She finally understood why her successful career left her wanting. Anna had awakened to the conflict between her spirit and her inherited inner rules. It was time to make a sacred choice.

Like Anna, as you awaken and grow spiritually, you will become aware of the conflicts inside of you that stand in the way of your life being how you want it to be. A conflict is an emotional and energetic disturbance caused by opposing ideas, as when Anna tried to live her life according to the tribe's rules rather than her spirit's path. Her tribal beliefs made her think she was happy, when energetically there wasn't a blip of happiness in her system.

Once they're firmly established, tribal laws shape your life without your awareness or input from your spirit.

- Tribal beliefs can cause you to forgive someone you don't forgive and make you confused about why you still react to that person or situation.
- Tribal beliefs can cause you to ignore guidance you knew was good for you because you are afraid of the changes it would require.
- Tribal beliefs can cause you to choose a life path you are certain you want, and then wonder why it doesn't fulfill you.
- Tribal beliefs can cause you to blame yourself when your life falls apart for no apparent reason.

This tug of war between your spirit and your limiting inner rules can last for years, leaving you wistfully yearning for more in life. The longer you try to be a good person and continually choose what the tribe has taught you, rather than what your heart longs for, the more disruption I find in your energy system.

This energy disturbance manifests as inner turmoil and will directly affect your feelings, stamina, and level of optimism. You feel trapped by the things you have to do, and guilty for not wanting to do them. This guilt morphs into a resentment you don't understand. As you work to ignore your unhappiness, you find yourself less energetic and go on autopilot as you live out someone else's life. You may even lose hope and become resigned to a way of life that pleases others but is at odds with your happiness. The playful part of you is so consumed by the rules of the tribe, you have forgotten how to play, how to laugh, how to be mischievous, and how to stay young. The possibilities for adventure and excitement become just a memory of your youth; you begin to feel older than you know you should, and begin to wonder what happened to the person you used to be. Thousands of Readings have taught me that many illnesses and problems, and much unhappiness, are caused by ignoring your spirit in favor of a tribe. It does not have to be this way. I watch people change their lives in an instant, and know that you can too.

Disturbances in your energy system will directly affect your feelings, stamina, and level of optimism.

To begin, you need to pay attention to the warning signs that a limiting belief is unconsciously driving your life away from your spirit:

- Do you frequently feel trapped? Do you relinquish new possibilities for your life because you feel trapped into doing things the "way they should be done"?
- Do you feel hindered in your ability to create the life you desire and deserve because your tribe doesn't agree with you?
- Do you feel defeated because just when you learn a spiritual lesson another one quickly follows?
- Do you feel older than you know you really are?
- Do you feel unable or prevented from living a fully spontaneous and honest life?
- Do you feel overwhelmed when you think about your future being the same as it is right now?

Limiting beliefs will curb your happiness by limiting your options in life.

In many families, it is understood that family matters should be kept private. As one client said to me, "What's cooked at home is eaten at home." But what happens if you are having problems within your marriage and need to talk to your best friend about it? Your tribal belief will make you either stuff your feelings, or talk with your friend but feel guilty about breaking the rules. Or, taught that only weak people believe in God, perhaps you long for a relationship with a Higher Power or God. You know that your life could be easier by simply accessing your guidance, yet you struggle with your desire to ask for help or pray because of a judgmental tribal influence.

These rules extend beyond your immediate family. In fact, some rules are so treasured by the mass consciousness—*because they seem so right and true*—they often turn into idiomatic expressions or clichés that have become an integral part of our communication. I am sure you have heard many such sayings as, "blood is thicker than water," "death before dishonor," "suffering is noble," or "when life gives you lemons, make lemonade."

These beliefs affect all arenas of life. For example, "no pain, no gain" is a common cliché with many interpretations, such as the obvious: when you exercise, if you do not sweat and push yourself, you will get no benefit from the workout. It could also mean that emotional pain is required to learn something new, or that achieving success or a promotion requires sacrifice. Consider the impact of such a belief on your life. You see, your beliefs become your thoughts and your thoughts shape your reality.

What is shaping your reality is a set of rules inherited from your family, religion, or culture, some of which are in conflict with what you *know* on a deep level is actually true. As my clairvoyant gifts developed, the rules from my religious tribe demanded that I shun them; however, my inner voice told me I could use my abilities to help others. This "knowing," what I call guidance or intuition, is a gift from God or a Higher Power.

When followed it will guide you unerringly and lovingly into your greatest happiness. It is the voice of your spirit, and following that voice is the best and quickest way to achieve long-lasting happiness in life.

> *Feeling torn is a sign that you are not completely sure that the tribal belief is true.*

Your guidance, or knowing, usually begins as a soft nudge and a whisper suggesting that life isn't the best it can be. Thoughts like "Does working so hard really make me a good person?," "I feel so tired after spending time with my friend; why do I hang on to the friendship?," "My husband is a great guy, so why do I feel so lonely around him?" are often ignored. Sometimes for a long time because we often mistake guidance for a debate and we negotiate with ourselves. In fact, it is a divine directive.

Perhaps you only mute the insistent urgings of your soul on certain big issues—like your significant relationship or your job. However, negotiating in any area moves you away from your spirit only to focus on your objections and fears. The longer you ignore a divine directive, the more out of balance you become. You begin to notice that nothing really excites you anymore, projects bore you, and your life becomes steady and uneventful.

You are losing your passion. Eventually, that initial whisper becomes a sonic boom. Your guidance becomes so loud, you must cover your eyes and ears to avoid it; this requires a tremendous outpouring of energy. This loss of energy leads to feeling unhappy, trapped, bored, depressed, burned out. In time, you may even feel physical symptoms like headaches and stomach pains.

Negotiating with your soul can lead to feeling:

Apathetic
Fatigued
Irritable
Unhappy
Loss of passion

Steadfastly ignoring your inner voice will lead to you feeling restless, dissatisfied, resentful, or depressed. While these symptoms may not seem severe, being bored and listless is not a healthy way to live. The prognosis for your life improving while ignoring what you know is quite poor. Your vibration lowers, your passion recedes, and your personal growth and spiritual evolution come to a screeching halt. One morning you wake up and ask: "Is this all there is?"

This serious imbalance of the mind, body, and spirit is what I call a flat-line existence or energetic suicide.

ENERGETIC SUICIDE

A state of energetic stagnation where there is minimal energy flow through the chakra system and a depressed vibration of one's energy field, often accompanied by vague physical symptoms without a definitive clinical diagnosis, and a lack of hope that one's life can change for the better.

People in energetic suicide feel exhausted, lost, and empty; are not fully present; have lost their passion and drive; and simply walk through the motions of life. This serious spiritual crisis demands your attention because your energy drops so drastically that it weakens your immune system and you unknowingly open yourself to all kinds of illness, such as severe allergies, arthritis, migraines, autoimmune disorders, diabetes, cancer, and heart disease.

This is the point at which people usually come to me. If their minds are open and willing, I can often help them heal unless they are too tired to continue living, or it is their time to die. Then there are those who *refuse to listen to what their soul wants for them;* I can do nothing for them. These people have chosen to stick with what they "know," to silence the urgent voice within and steer their lives instead by the old, deep-rooted thinking of their family, their religion, or their culture—even if they are steering themselves right into their grave.

Fortunately, guidance doesn't simply go away because you ignore it. The soul is very persistent in wanting your happiness.

I wrote this book so you can avoid a flat-line existence and re-claim your passion. My abilities have been described as a "megaphone for your soul." *You already know what is best for you;* I am going to help you hear it more clearly and more loudly by helping you become aware of your deep-seated internal rules that silence that voice. You need only be willing to explore, chal-lenge, and change the ideas that limit your happiness.

A belief at odds with your spirit can help you age faster.

I call these ingrained ideas "tribal beliefs" because they are taught to you by the various tribes you are a part of. Who are these tribes? They are the social groups or institutions you be-long to: your family of origin, your ancestors, your religion, your school, your workplace, your part of the country, your na-tion, and so on. Tribal beliefs are based on what has worked for the tribe in the past (perhaps even the far distant past). As each new member comes along, the tribe instills its beliefs into them, passing along the tribe's values and its knowledge of how life works. No one is exempt from this process. Every single one of us has been taught countless tribal beliefs, whether we are con-scious of them or not. These tribal beliefs can be very subtle and are even found in commercials on television. Sometimes rooted in a nugget of truth, these long-standing ideas become a way of life one comes to expect, such as:

Love requires sacrifice.

Suffering is noble.

Change is hard.

Worrying is a way of showing people you love them.

Grieving for a lifetime means you really loved the
person.

Don't say something negative or be honest if it will
hurt someone's feelings.

Each tribal belief also carries a subtext—a powerful energetic, unspoken message—that can seriously alter your life. For
example, the tribal belief *If I'm good, God will love me* carries the
powerful punch that if bad things happen in your life, you must
be bad. If a tragedy occurs in your life, you will reflexively judge
yourself, and this harshness can destroy your self-esteem, diminish your ability or desire to accept love from others, and ultimately make you feel unworthy, ashamed, and deserving of
punishment by God. This subtle but powerful subtext is often
reflected in a person's painful lament: "What did I do to deserve
this?"

And that's the power of a single tribal belief from just one of your tribes!

Some of the stories you'll read in this book about people
changing their limiting beliefs have such wonderful outcomes,
they may sound like fairy tales. They are all true, and they all
began with people being willing to accept themselves as they

truly were, not as the person they (or someone else) thought they should be.

Let me tell you about Debra. When I first met her, I saw a passionate, smart, mischievous, and wickedly funny woman with one of the brightest lights shining inside her. But a terrible gray film was covering Debra's vibrant energy. While I "saw" this gray film energetically, it was also an apt metaphor for her life. Debra was covering up her considerable gifts as a graphic designer at a big advertising agency. She was promoted within six months but neglected to share that accomplishment with her husband, Bill, and she rarely mentioned the attention her work was garnering. Debra had two tribal beliefs causing a conflict within her soul:

- A woman should never outshine her husband.
- It's not okay to blow your own horn or acknowledge your talents—the subtext is be humble; nobody likes a braggart.

She could have continued downplaying her abilities, except she developed asthmalike symptoms that kept her at home struggling to breathe. Her breathing problems were directly related to her conflict: her soul needed to expand and use and enjoy her artistic talents, but it was being constricted by her loyalty to her limiting beliefs.

Thus, on a deep level Debra agrees with her tribe that her success at work is wrong. This is where the conflict with her soul (and that gray shroud that surrounds her) began. Things got worse when Bill began attacking Debra and fighting with her about her success. She might have drawn the line with him at that point—except she was afraid it would end her marriage and she was also taught *If your marriage ends, you are a loser.*

So Debra was temporarily stuck between a rock and a hard place—always an indication that a tribal belief is warring with your soul. Debra believed she had to either give up her art to make her marriage work or excel professionally, making her a loser.

Sadly, I agree with her. Debra *is* a loser—a loser of life, joy, happiness, success, and laughter. She is also losing touch with her soul, day by day, and that is sadder than any words can express. Debra could change those tribal beliefs overnight. (I'll show you how to do this in Chapter 6.) I suggested that she consider alternative possibilities such as:

> It is reasonable to believe that when you acknowledge your talents, you are acknowledging the gifts God has given you.
>
> It is reasonable to believe that a wife's happiness contributes richly to her marriage.
>
> It is reasonable to believe that sometimes wonderful people end up in marriages that end.

As you can see, coming up with new tribal beliefs is a creative endeavor that comes from an open mind. Debra recognized the link between her suffocating breaths and her limiting beliefs and chose to change them. She chose to honor herself, acknowledge her gifts, and risk her marriage. By respecting herself and her abilities and allowing herself to excel, she changed the dynamic of her relationship with her husband. She stopped apologizing for who she was and taught him to respect her. Last I heard, she was chosen to manage the entire art department and her husband proudly sat next to her at the promotion dinner.

Kudos to Debra; now how about you? I know you have things in your life that you are struggling with because you have chosen to pick up this book. I am here to tell you that you do not have to struggle anymore, even if you believe that *Struggling is an inherent part of life.* I will show you how simple it can be to identify the tribal beliefs that are blocking your path to success and happiness, and how quickly you can change them. When you bring your beliefs into true alignment with your soul, you experience *immediate* personal change and the payoff is fantastic. You will feel great—full of energy, glowing with happiness, brimming with new ideas! People will ask if you lost weight, fell in love, won the lottery, or found a miracle drug.

The answer, of course, is much, much simpler.

You chose to explore, challenge, and change a limiting belief at odds with your inner knowledge, to consider a new possibility, and to listen to your innermost needs. You had the courage to "think outside the tribe" and listen to the urgings of your soul. You made the *sacred choice* to honor your spirit and trust where it would lead you.

For each tribal belief that stands in the way of your vibrant health and happiness, you'll ask yourself the following questions:

- Do I feel like I'm between a rock and a hard place?
- What is my spirit whispering to me?
- What do I know that I don't want to know?

- Can I honor my spirit and take care of myself, even though it goes against my tribal belief?
- Am I willing to trust the voice of my spirit—my guidance, intuition, knowing?
- Am I willing to take a risk? Even though people say the world is flat, am I willing to listen to my spirit and maybe discover that it is round?

When making a *sacred choice* becomes your guiding principle, you will find yourself happier than you ever imagined. I have seen this happen again and again with my clients. Helping you do the same is what this book is about.

We'll start by taking a good look at the two opposing sides in the struggle for your allegiance: your tribal belief and your soul. You'll learn how tribes work and why they can be so fierce in their demands for loyalty. Then I'll teach you about the soul. You'll learn how the soul communicates with us, how to discover what your soul wants for you, and, most important, how to distinguish the inner voice of your soul from the internalized voice of the tribe.

Next we'll focus on identifying the limiting tribal beliefs that are underlying—and driving—your life. I'll show you four simple ways to uncover the exact beliefs that are blocking your health and happiness. Once you have a list of these beliefs before you, I'll teach you a quick process for changing each one. We'll pay special attention to any "showstopper" beliefs you might have (like *Change is hard*). I'll walk you through the same method I use with clients and students to create new beliefs that will enable you to soar, making you an inspiration to all who know you.

By the end of this book, you'll know better which tribal beliefs have been keeping you from the health and happiness you deserve. You'll have a list of them in black and white, and you'll understand the specific impact each has had on your life. Best of all, you'll have a Tribal Log of spiritually based beliefs to pass on to the next generation, you will further your spiritual growth, and raise the overall vibration of our planet.

Now let's get started. I want *you* to be wildly happy and passionate as soon as possible!

2.

The Awesome Power of a Tribal Belief

CHANGING YOUR LIMITING TRIBAL
BELIEFS CAN INSTANTLY HEAL
AN EMOTIONAL, PHYSICAL,
OR SPIRITUAL ISSUE

By now you are probably excited by the prospect of taking charge of your life and living according to your spirit. While making this choice will bring you genuine, long-lasting happiness, you may find yourself at odds with your tribe—people you trust and look up to, people you have depended upon to teach you right from wrong.

I wrote this book to help you learn to listen to your spirit. The purpose of *Sacred Choices* is to explore your tribal beliefs and determine if they are good for you—to decide whether they raise or lower your vibration. Some tribal beliefs cause you distress and can lower your overall energy and even cause illness. The idea is to be aware of your unconscious choices—to become more conscious and thereby have a greater role in living your life the way you want it to be—not how you were taught, or how you believe it's supposed to be.

> *Listening to your spirit filters out the beliefs that lower your energy and cause you conflict.*

When you decide to heed the call of your soul, you can't assume your tribe will be happy about it. Sometimes, change scares people. Although it seems like a paradox—that the people who love you might not celebrate your good fortune—it makes sense when you look at the nature and purpose of tribes.

The key purpose of a tribe is protection. The cave dwellers needed to pool their skills and energy to hunt down large animals, keep the fire going, get cared for when they were ill, and protect themselves from unfriendly neighbors. In those days, a person without a tribe usually died from starvation or attack. Tribal beliefs served to keep the group together and keep everyone safe: *Never turn your back on a woolly mammoth!* It was a huge risk to try a new way of hunting, for example, when you only had one shot at the woolly mammoth. If your new way failed, the tribe would starve.

Remember the tribe's reaction when Ayla in Jean Auel's novel *Clan of the Cave Bear* learned to use a slingshot? Women were forbidden to use any type of weapon. Even though she saved the chief's son from a wild animal attack, she was shunned from her tribe. Normally, she would have been put to death, but in recognition of saving the boy's life, they simply made her dead. They could no longer see her or hear her and she wasn't allowed to be with her young son or stay with the tribe. The tribe turned its back on her.

At first glance, this seems a terrible repercussion for not listening to her tribe. However, being forced out on her own caused her to redouble her resourcefulness and meet others from different tribes. Combining their knowledge led to a new way of life that was easier. Meanwhile, Ayla's old clan died out from stagnant living, or a static way of life.

INSPIRATION

The fire that drives us to greatness requires looking beyond what we know—to consider excitingly different possibilities.

Our evolution demands that we be dynamic, not static thinkers, and inspiration, the fire that drives us to greatness, requires us to look beyond what we know and consider new possibilities. This inspiration, what I call divine vision, can come anytime, anywhere, and should not be ignored.

In mid-December, I was speeding in the early morning to the trauma center to begin a twelve-hour shift. From nowhere a blue car was suddenly on my rear bumper before dangerously passing me and narrowly missing the side of my car. As I sharply swerved, my tire blew out; at seventy miles per hour,

I came close to losing control of my car as I tried to avoid an accident.

I mumbled an expletive surveying a very flat tire, knowing I would be late for work. Hands greasy and thirty minutes late, I arrived in the emergency room to a tumultuous and chaotic scene. Three teams of doctors and nurses were working feverishly on a two-year-old, a nine-year-old, and a thirty-four-year-old woman involved in an accident. I worked with the nine-year-old and learned that a drunk driver had careened into the family van, sending them into a cement wall.

It was a brutal way to begin the morning. The nine-year-old and the mother died. The two-year-old was sent up to surgery. I thought about my experience on the road that morning and realized how lucky I had been. Then my self-righteousness took over and I had just started to mentally harangue the reckless driver from my morning encounter, when I recognized the driver of the blue car. He was slumped on the floor crying with his face in his hands.

My tirade ended abruptly as I realized he had been racing to the ER to see his family who had been in a terrible accident. It was a moment of clarity for me as I realized how narrow my vision could be at times. When I looked farther than two feet in front of my nose, I saw that he was not a reckless driver, but rather, a terrified husband and father racing to protect his family. My anger evaporated into compassion as I sat with him and prayed. I also prayed for myself and vowed to look beyond what my human eyes could see, and focus on a larger or divine picture.

RIPPLE EFFECT

The ongoing energy and impact of our decisions, beliefs, and choices on others—long after the initial choice was made.

I learned the essence of divine vision—to see the ripple effect of our actions, thoughts, and words. I learned firsthand about the interconnectedness of our human race, how my actions and thoughts can affect the world around me. I took responsibility that day for all that I broadcast into the world. Like the flutter of a butterfly's wings in Japan that results in a wave on the Pacific Coast, my small act of annoyance could create a big impact. I humbly recognized the essence of the power we all own.

Power is neutral and can be used to create love or hate, ease or struggle. When I teach about the ripple effect, people are astounded. When you come to realize how powerful a being you are, your life can change in an instant. You can have an impact on what is happening in the world—simply by choosing the energy that you broadcast.

Such vision allows a tribe to evolve. Ayla understood the ripple effect of her actions. She knew that using that slingshot would anger her tribe. But she took a risk for a greater good. When you consider changing your limiting beliefs, you display courage.

While the woolly mammoth may have died out, the fear and the need to belong to a tribe have not. Most people want to belong to a tribe; it brings comfort to share common beliefs and have an identity. The stronger your tribe, the safer you feel. Again, it's all about survival.

The human need to belong to a group is primal. You can see just how strong this drive is when you read about a highly intelligent woman who ends up in a cult or hear about a wealthy man who doesn't realize that his so-called friends are just along for the free ride. You can see it, too, in children who get into gangs and lonely people who join faddish, even self-destructive, groups.

Belonging to a tribe also helps us make sense of the world. Because each tribe has its own set of tribal beliefs and traditions that define it, you know where you stand, whether the tribe is a social club that does not allow single women, a secret brotherhood with a special handshake, or the office staff who expects you to chip in for every coworker's birthday (whether you like them or not!). When you belong to a group, you wake up each morning and can count on your tribe's rules to create order in a sometimes-chaotic world. You know what to wear, you know how to act, you know what's expected of you.

Before we go any further, I want to stress that not all tribal beliefs are bad for you. You don't have to reject a belief just because your tribe taught it to you. What I think you do have to do is become aware of each tribal belief you are living by (I'll walk you through how to do this in Chapters 5 and 6), then ask yourself whether it enhances your life or not. Is that belief in alignment with your soul? Do you feel good—*really good*—

about following this rule? If so, keep it! If not, however, ask yourself if you can consider another possibility. Too often I see people clinging to beliefs that are not in their highest good. Is it possible that some of the beliefs that you, too, were taught are not best for your spirit?

People often ask me, "Why would my parents teach me things that aren't good for me?" For the most part, your parents were simply trying to protect you and prepare you for life by teaching you their values and their own inherited ideas about how life works. By instilling tribal beliefs in you, they were telling you what the tribe considered appropriate behavior, expected behavior, and desired behavior. They learned these beliefs from their parents. Unfortunately, fear can be the root of a tribal belief.

For example, many of our ancestors were dramatically affected by war: World War I, World War II, the Korean War, the Cold War, and the Vietnam War. As a result, many of their beliefs are based on fear, distrust, and world unrest. Some of our parents and grandparents grew up during the Depression, when work was hard to find. They taught us to get a good job and keep it no matter what. They taught us to buy a house and get it paid off as soon as possible (if you had a mortgage, you might miss payments and be foreclosed on). They taught their daughters that they had to get married to have financial security and happiness, because opportunities for women were more limited back then.

These Depression-era beliefs and fears revolve around the issue of security (*The rug can be pulled out at any minute*). They are rooted in a scarcity consciousness (*There will never be enough*) and result in a tremendous need to horde and hold on to things (clutter consciousness). These rules made sense, given the experiences our parents or grandparents encountered: the stock market *did* crash overnight. But beliefs and subsequent rules, once in place, tend to solidify and be passed down as fact.

And these rules made sense according to Maslow's hierarchy of needs; safety is the primary need of any human being. Without it, we cannot focus on anything else. Remember that many tribals were originally designed to provide a form of safety. But as more of our safety needs are met, these older rules become constricting to our spirit.

Tribal beliefs can also contribute to misunderstandings and plain old hurtfulness. If the tribe defines someone as "manly" if he is an excited football enthusiast, what happens to the son who doesn't like contact sports and has an expressive, quiet, and artistic nature? If the tribe defines someone as "womanly" if she is sensitive, caretaking, and a mother who stays at home, what happens to the strong-minded and independent daughter who chooses the military or law as a career? Until we examine and reconsider these hurtful tribal beliefs and teach our children differently, it will be the way of the world. People often wonder about their purpose in life. Consider passing on a belief system to your children that promotes tolerance and understanding.

Because tribal beliefs are what define a tribe—thus keeping it intact and safe—no one is happy when somebody starts thinking outside the tribe. I ran into this when I was an ER nurse. Sometimes I would moonlight at other ERs, where I was able to pick up some great ideas—and stub my toe on some antiquated ones. Each hospital had its own rules,

which were made plain to newcomers. If a rule proved ineffi-
cient and I questioned it, the response was always the same:
"Well, this is how we do it in this ER." The message was clear:
don't buck the tribe—even if the new way will improve things
dramatically.

However, the ER is one place where rules often have to be
ignored in the heat of the moment. If we did not have a chest
tube that would fit a patient, we modified an existing one—
even though you were not allowed to use any "new" equipment
unless it had been approved by multiple hospital committees. If
very young children were not allowed to visit a hospitalized parent, but we knew it would be healing for both of them, we
snuck the toddlers in. One snowy night at 2 A.M. when we were
starving but the cafeteria was closed and no restaurant would
deliver, we broke a big rule by getting some patient food and
eating it quietly in the back room. The rules were clear: the staff
was *not* allowed to eat patient food. It didn't matter that having
no snacks or meals during a twelve-hour shift would make the
nurses hungry, cranky, and dizzy from low blood sugar and
would impair their decision-making skills. A law was a law and
meant to be adhered to! Apparently, we were known as the "bad
girls" of the hospital because our rules did not always match the
administration's rules. Luckily, a blind eye was usually turned
to our actions because the ends—saving a life—justified the
means. Sometimes other members of a tribe recognize the need
for change but don't know how or are afraid to begin. Like the
chief of Ayla's tribe, our supervisor understood the need to
bend the tribal rules. She knew we needed to eat on occasion
while at work but knew she would never win her case with hos-

pital administration. Her solution? She ordered several "patient" trays just before the kitchen closed and asked us to hide them in the nurses' lounge where we could eat unobserved. We were very grateful to her. You, too, can make a difference by following your "knowing."

Even though we no longer live in caves, the continuance of the tribe still depends on its members more or less following the rules. If enough people start thinking on their own, the tribe will certainly change and, at times, may even disband. The tribe finds this discomforting, frightening, and very, very threatening. For example, in 1633, Galileo faced the Inquisition for his heretical belief that the earth revolved around the sun. He was found guilty and required to recant his ideas, publication of his work—including any future work—was forbidden, and he spent the last nine years of his life under house arrest.

However, consider the inhabitants of Lake Titicaca, located high in the Andes on the border of Peru and Bolivia. They grow up on floating islands and leave their family to float on their own. When they find people of like-mindedness, they connect their reed islands and form a new tribe. *Thinking outside the tribe allows us to evolve and form new tribes to exchange ideas, further our development, and nurture our spirits.*

When Albert realized his patrol partner, Charlie, was stealing from people they arrested, he was very distressed. Diagnosed with an inflammation of his stomach lining, he alternated be-

tween being tense and angry. Torn between loyalty to his partner of fourteen years and his personal code of ethics, Albert
kept silent at first. When a trip to the emergency room revealed
high blood pressure, Albert realized that his joy at fulfilling his
dream of being a police officer had turned into a nightmare. He
was going to have to talk to his partner.

> *Thinking outside your tribe opens the door to inspiration.*

When Albert spoke to Charlie, his partner rationalized the
stealing and refused to stop. Albert's tribal belief *Be loyal to a good
friend, no matter what* had him trapped in an untenable situation.
Charlie had helped Albert during a rough time, and for that,
Albert felt indebted to him. The only two options he saw were
to be disloyal to himself (and the oath he took as a policeman)
or to betray his friend, and he wouldn't betray his friend. I suggested a third option.

I asked Albert to listen quietly to his spirit. "Does Charlie
deserve your loyalty and friendship?" I could see the answer immediately in Albert's field, along with the conflict that swirled
around him. He acknowledged that time alone did not create a
bond between them, but rather mutual respect and trust. Albert
had neither for Charlie and recognized that the friendship had
begun to end nearly three years earlier.

Together we began to rewrite his tribal belief. Albert came
up with several that were in alignment with his spirit:

- It's reasonable to believe that there are appropriate times to question one's loyalty to a friend, especially when that loyalty requires going against your ethics.
- It's reasonable to believe that a friend can do things to lose your loyalty.
- It's reasonable to believe that loyalty to a friend should not put you between a rock and hard place.

Albert decided to end his friendship and partnership with Charlie. He also told him of his profound discomfort with his behavior and that it had led to the destruction of their friendship, and asked him to stop. As he began to live a life based on his new beliefs, his blood pressure returned to normal and his stomach healed. His wife is thrilled because his constant tension and anger have evaporated.

Those of us who have the courage to challenge unhealthy tribal beliefs are performing an important service: like all forms of life, a tribe must adapt to changes in its environment or circumstances, or it will die out. This is the very nature of evolution. Consider the Knights of the Round Table—their "tribe" died out because of its inability to change. It lived by the rules of chivalry. This meant that when the knights fought, they allowed their enemies time to get up when they were knocked to the ground. They fought like civilized men. However, the invasion of the Saxons (who were considered barbarians) created many challenges for the knights. The Saxons threw sand in their eyes and took advantage of a knight who had fallen to the ground. They did not fight with civility.

> *Your loyalties can go to your limiting beliefs or your potential.*

The knights faced a true dilemma: Should they remain loyal to their chivalrous laws or learn to adapt to their new enemy? The strength of chivalric law was so great that many loyal knights fell to the Saxons' blades feeling angry, bewildered, and betrayed because the barbarians had broken the rules. (Even the few knights who learned to fight differently and survived felt debased for abandoning their ideals.) In the same way, your office colleagues will feel angry and betrayed when you break the rules by refusing to donate for a gift for someone you do not like. They might even think you are an ignorant barbarian!

I have rarely seen a tribe who celebrates a new way of thinking—rather, tribe members become scared, angry, and sometimes resentful. The same holds true for every one of your tribes, whether it's your family, bowling league, office clutch, church assembly, or circle of friends. There are very clear rules and when you buck them, there will be no celebration for your higher thinking. People will be shocked, angered, saddened, but mostly scared. So please don't get discouraged when your tribe neglects to delight in your newfound freedom or forgets to bake you a cake. Your spirit will celebrate with you as you become an inspiration for others.

If there were no risk takers, no dreamers, no explorers, no people like Christopher Columbus, would the human race have moved forward in any area of achievement? Of course visionary thinking threatens the tightly knit structure of the tribe. People are scared for themselves *and for you.* Remember the contempt that the European art establishment first felt for the impressionists? One influential critic, writing in the newspaper *La Presse,* declared, "The excesses of this school sicken or disgust." I think what he was really saying was, if all painters begin working impressionistically, what will happen to successful art teachers, experts, and critics like me? We will become obsolete. Then *we* will have to decide whether to stay in the realm of the safe and familiar, or challenge the establishment!

When someone starts thinking outside the tribe, it is often misinterpreted as "the old way is no good." But it's not about branding as good or bad. It's not even about rejecting the tribe. It's about changing your life for the better, living your life according to the needs of your soul. At first, it is a difficult choice. You feel as though you must betray your tribe or betray your soul. The truth is, no matter what your tribe members think, you will *not* be betraying them. You don't need to convince them that your way is better. Rather, be a program of attraction rather than promotion as they say in the twelve-step program. You will be a role model for spiritual evolution and living the way God intended you to live.

Abby was confronted with a choice like this the morning she received a call from her church reminding her to renew the payment for her father's memorial plaque. While nothing was said overtly, there was a strong assumption (a tribal belief) that she should pony up to keep the plaque as proof that she continued to mourn for her father and honor his memory. Abby's soul rebelled at the idea. Her father, who was known publicly as an observant and religious man, had been a menace in the home. He was ruled by his rage and his children paid the price. One time he got so angry at Abby's younger brother, he did not speak a word to the child for six months!

Abby was faced with a difficult choice: to continue the charade of honoring her emotionally abusive father or to follow the call of her soul and donate the money instead to prevent child abuse. She thought it over and made a sacred choice to honor her spirit rather than tribal law: she declined to renew the memorial plaque and, with a big smile on her face, wrote a check to her local child-abuse prevention center.

Mentioning Abby's abusive father brings up an important point. Even people who have hurt you when you were young can teach you tribal beliefs. For example, abusers often tell children or spouses that the abuse is their fault. Many adults suffer with the belief that they were responsible for being abused or molested. You can imagine how detrimental such a tribal belief can be.

While many tribal laws are at least *intended* to help you succeed in life, others may have been inculcated in you for purely selfish motives. If you had an emotionally immature parent who put his or her own needs before those of the children, or if you were raised (or strongly influenced) by someone who was narcissistic, had a martyr complex, or had some other psychological problem, you were probably taught to stand in that person's shadow. Parents (or teachers or religious leaders or other authority figures) like this are only interested in their own needs, not yours. Imagine if you were taught to honor your mother or father, no matter what.

> *Sharing the same bloodline does not afford privileges to undermine and injure.*

Take Karen, for example. As a child, Karen was repeatedly taught *Be respectful and good to your parents, especially if they are old or sick.* Now an adult, she allows her elderly mother to get away with behavior she would not normally tolerate from anyone else in her life. Karen's mother sees herself as a martyr but does not suffer in silence. In fact, she generally calls a family press conference to announce her distress. Karen tolerates these tirades and rudeness because her mother is her only remaining parent, she's over eighty years old, and she is unwell.

But Karen is also unwell. She's trying to heal from cancer. She once led a very disciplined life: eat, sleep, work, and follow the rules. Then she contracted a deadly type of cancer and assumed she would die of it. The disease was progressing until one day when she decided she didn't want to die! She consulted me and I told her that 90 to 95 percent of her attention had to be focused on her healing in order to get well. This meant taking care of herself and resolving conflicts. Karen began to explore and rewrite the tribal beliefs that were in conflict with her spirit and were draining her energy. She took some time off to enjoy life. She blossomed and began enjoying trips and personal endeavors that brought her joy.

She visited her mother less often. Being around her mother's martyr energy truly drained Karen, and she could not afford that. Now her mother's tirades were even more dreadful, and Karen felt herself starting to succumb to her mother's demands to spend more time with her. After all, her old tribal belief required her to be good to older people *at all costs.* Then one day, Karen's mother noticed her daughter was not only taking trips and having fun, she was getting well. Was her mother happy about that? No!

"What do you mean, you're full of energy?" she demanded. "You are supposed to be sick!" Not only had Karen bucked the tribe by starting to heal (according to Western medicine, her type of cancer was fatal), she had put her own need to heal ahead of her mother's need for a constant audience for her complaints. Karen was so shocked by her mother's selfish words, she immediately renewed her commitment to her new tribal belief *(Focus on my healing at all costs),* curtailed her visits, and got back on her path to recovery.

Ignoring the voice of your spirit can have profound repercussions. In the sixties, Stanley Milgram conducted classic experiments on obedience to authority.[1] Volunteers known as the teachers were told to ask questions of study participants called learners in the adjacent room (whom they couldn't see, but could hear). Each time learners gave the incorrect answer to a question, the teacher was to punish them with a small electric shock, beginning with 45 volts. For every wrong answer, the voltage was increased by 15 volts.

The teachers believed that for each wrong answer, the learner was receiving actual shocks. In reality, there were no shocks. A tape recorder integrated with the electroshock generator played prerecorded sounds for each shock level. After a number of voltage-level increases, the learner started to bang on the wall, complaining about his heart condition. He then gave no further response to the questions and made no further complaints.

At this point many people indicated their desire to stop the experiment and check on the learner. Some teachers paused at 135 volts and began to question the purpose of the experiment. Some continued after being assured that they would not be held responsible. Some participants began to laugh nervously once they heard the screams of pain coming from the learner. If at any time the teachers indicated their desire to halt the experiment, they were given a succession of verbal prods by the experimenter, in this order:

---

[1] The experiment was first described by Stanley Milgram, a psychologist at Yale University, in an article titled "Behavioral Study of Obedience" published in the *Journal of Abnormal and Social Psychology* in 1963.

1. Please continue.
2. The experiment requires you to continue, please go on.
3. It is essential that you continue.
4. You have no choice, you must continue.

At times the stress and conflict of the *teachers* was so great they broke down and wept, but they continued to administer electric shocks. If the teacher still wished to stop after all four successive verbal prods, the experiment was halted. Otherwise, it was halted after the teacher had given the learner the maximum 450-volt shock three times in succession.

To the immense relief of the volunteers, when the study was concluded they were told that no real shocks were given. When asked why they continued to hurt the learners—even when they screamed in pain, the response was generally the same: because someone in authority (researcher in a white lab coat) told them to do it. Their limiting tribal belief to obey authority was so great, they twisted their guts and their souls into a knot to obey. They went against their humanness—even their empathy and compassion were not enough to override their powerful beliefs about authority.

If you think this couldn't be you, think again. I watch people twist their guts and spirit all the time. That's the power of an unconscious limiting belief.

SYMPTOMOLOGY

*When you ignore the urgings of your spirit and you
violate your soul one small piece at a time,
your body will bear the brunt.*

When you give in to the tyranny of the tribe and ignore the urging of your spirit, you violate your soul one small piece at a time—and this is not good for your health. Vague symptoms crop up, you notice you aren't as happy as you used to be, and you don't have the energy you once had. Eventually your life becomes quite uncomfortable until the numbness begins to take over. This disconnection from your spirit is the beginning of the end of passion and verve. You live within a tribe similar to the Borg from *Star Trek*—a collective of beings who think exactly alike, have no personal thoughts or feelings, or connection with their spirit. They simply follow the rules. Their prime directive is the survival of the tribe. By getting others to think and act like them, the tribe stays strong, but the individual spirit all but disappears.

Let me show you step by step how this works. Let's say that you have always dreamed of having someone to really love, someone who would really love you. Maybe your grandparents had a very happy marriage and you remember it with high hopes for yourself. When you grow up and start looking for a partner, however, people begin telling you that a good relationship takes work. Your parents say so, your friends say so, and you have heard it on TV or read it in a book about how to find a mate. So you believe it. And your strong belief sets you up to attract a partner who will be a lot of work. (I'll explain exactly how this works in the next chapter.)

Fortunately, your soul knows better. Your soul knows you *can* have a relationship like your grandparents', one that's fun and easy! Your soul wants you to find a partner who brings you joy every day, who delights in your love and laughter, and who also believes that a good relationship can be easy. This sets up a conflict between what you believe (and are therefore willing to allow in your life) and what your soul wants for you. Conflict with your spirit always takes its toll. It takes energy to ignore the call of your spirit. It drains you and weakens your system.

One day you meet someone you are attracted to. You date, you fall in love, and you see your dream coming true, even though it can be hard to get along with the person at times—you fight, have different temperaments and interests, and don't much like each other's friends. Instead of dating other people, though, you persevere in trying to make your new relationship work. That takes even more energy.

Eventually you get engaged to this person. The relationship continues to be a lot of work, but as long as you give in most of the time, it's still a good relationship. Right? Pretty soon you start to notice some troubling symptoms. Sometimes your vision blurs, and often you are tired. You chalk it up to your hectic schedule. Maybe you get a tingling or numbness in your hands and feet. Minor stuff, you think, nothing to worry about. So you marry, start a family, and continue to struggle with trying to have the wonderful relationship that you saw your grandparents enjoy. Your dream isn't coming true, though, and unbeknownst to you, your symptoms start moving toward full-blown illness. The years go by, the kids are now in school, and your marriage continues to take a lot of effort to stay on course. *Nothing* seems to be easy about it. But long ago you resigned yourself to the hard work "required" by a good relationship, so you hang in there, even though you feel sort of trapped and unhappy. Then one day your doctor diagnoses you with lupus. (One of the energetic precursors to autoimmune disorders is an inability—refusal or otherwise—to enjoy life. Additionally, with lupus, there is the feeling of being trapped with no way out.)

Survival and safety are core needs for human beings, and we are used to getting these needs met by sticking with our tribes. There's another way to achieve safety and ensure your survival though. Give up the tribal beliefs that keep you separated from your soul, from the voice of God within you.

When you adhere to a tribal belief that is hurting you, when you emotionally defend it and cling to it, your spirit inevitably suffers. After a time, the violation of your spirit becomes more pronounced, but easier to accept. Eventually the disconnection with your soul becomes automatic and unconscious, and your mind, body, and spirit are out of balance; perhaps you even develop some sort of illness. I'll show you exactly how this progression works in the next chapter when we talk about the other contender for your loyalty: your shining soul.

If you wish to live harmoniously with your soul, you must examine those tribal beliefs that limit your happiness and choose for yourself what is right for you. Your choice should be based on the spiritual voice inside of you—not simply what you were taught is true. For example, while it sounds true that hard work is the way to reap financial rewards, the truth is, it is not always true or necessary.

Some tribes can help you listen to the voice of your soul; some cannot. It doesn't matter. Becoming aware of your tribal beliefs will begin the process of giving your spirit a voice. Simply put, listening to that voice means making a sacred choice to do and believe things because they make your heart sing!

Your sacred responsibility is to honor your spirit and make choices that eliminate conflict so that you can get on with your true purpose in life.

3.

The Tenacity of Your Spirit

HEEDING THE WHISPER
OF YOUR SPIRIT
WILL LEAD YOU
TO A GREAT LIFE

If you made a choice to heed the advice of your soul, your life would change in a dramatically positive way. Unfortunately, the opposite is also true.

There is no problem living according to the tribal beliefs you were taught if these beliefs are in alignment with your soul. But sometimes they are not. The beliefs that cramp your life and stunt your joy are not always so obvious. Just because your life looks great on the outside doesn't mean you aren't in conflict on the inside. Imagine you are a doctor who has a young family and a busy job in a downtown hospital, who is not listening to her soul. Everyone is proud of what you have made of your life—including you, but you aren't happy. Now ask yourself, What if . . .

Your parents say . . . a good daughter makes a success of herself by becoming a professional—(subtext: writing is not a profession).

But your soul says, I want to write.

Your ancestors say . . . if you don't work hard, you won't get anywhere in life—(subtext: writing is not real work).

But your soul says, I want to write.

Your colleagues say . . . everyone here works a sixty-hour week—(subtext: if you want to fit in, play by our rules).

But your soul says, I want to write.

You tend to pay attention to your body and your mind, but what about your spirit? You know, that little voice inside of you, the one that whispers those ideas that, when followed, change your life in a miraculous way. It's also that little voice inside that can scare you because it is a harbinger of great change that you might not be ready to accept. And that's why it's so easy to ignore it! Especially when you can rationalize ignoring your spirit in favor of honoring your tribe.

Now that we've looked at the nature of tribes, I think you can understand why, if your spirit alerts you to a tribal belief that is thwarting your success, happiness, and spiritual growth, you might not rush to change it. First, you might not even recognize that it's a tribal belief, because sometimes, your tribe's laws are taught by actions, not words, and therefore seem like the way things are. Second, sometimes you are afraid to change.

Take Don, a hardworking twenty-seven-year-old single guy

who is working late and playing hard. During childhood, he watched his father work two jobs for most of his life until his death at age fifty-seven. Once, Don asked him why he worked so hard, and his dad shrugged. "That's what men do." An innocuous comment that Don barely remembered did not form his tribal belief, but rather, the trapped and resigned feeling that emanated from his dad. It was the unspoken rule that a good man works his tail off and provides everything for his family, and does not waste time with frivolous things like play.

Don loves to hike and bike and enjoys nature, but he doesn't allow himself these luxuries unless he has worked very hard all week. He puts in extra hours and takes on large projects to earn the right to play. He proves that he is a good man, and only then can he hit the trails. This conflict eventually sidelined him with a diagnosis of fibromyalgia. He learned early on that it wasn't okay to enjoy life—he was supposed to work. Even after his father's death, Don tried to live up to his legacy.

> *When you feel trapped, your body gets angry.*

We got to work quickly on rewriting his tribal beliefs about being a man, hard work, and being a provider for a family. He began to notice how he "kept score" to earn his fun and rewrote his limiting beliefs around play. He was pleasantly shocked when his mother broke down in tears when he shared his new *Aha* with her. She had lost her husband because of his need to work and was sick with worry as she watched Don start down the same path. When she tried to talk to him about it, he simply wouldn't consider her pleas. The fibromyalgia slowed him down long enough to reconsider the possibility that there might be a different way to live his life, be a good man, and enjoy his life. He now works for an outdoor adventure company leading tours and loves it!

AHA

A moment of clarity or knowing when you understand the priorities of your life.

The third reason you might not rush out to change a limiting belief is because, unlike Don's mother, not all families will celebrate your newfound freedom and happiness. Remember what happened when you strolled home twenty minutes past your curfew? Was there a celebration? Probably not. More likely you were made aware of your parents' displeasure.

Many tribal beliefs are meant to keep us safe, but there is a difference between being safe because you are following the rules, and being safe because you are following your soul. When you break the tribal rules, such as *Be respectful of authority,* you feel like you've done something wrong. Question an authority figure like a teacher, a priest, or your doctor? No way, says your tribe. Some tribes will adhere so strongly to this belief, they will fight for it, and yes, some will even die for it. Your compliance with this law is overseen by the people who not only shelter you, but command and confer such things as approval, love, status, and other worldly temptations. But what about when your spirit is nudging you to ask the question?

Once you have heard your spirit and recognized a limiting tribal belief, what will you choose? Can you break from tribal tradition and listen to the voice of your soul? At first glance, this can be a daunting proposition because you can't consider an alternative way. But only at first glance. In reality, your soul is also enormously powerful—more powerful than any tribe. Your soul is connected to the greatest energy in the universe. It is the part of you most like God or your Higher Power. Your soul will never lead you in the wrong direction. To tap into the divine energy of your soul at any moment, you need only notice and respond to its signals. I call it *synchrodivinity*, thanks to a wonderful and amazing woman in Sun Valley, Idaho. It means that everything we need, everything we need to know, is waiting for us if we would simply take the time to listen. It's that simple. Look at Don. When I initially asked him if he could have fun and work hard at the same time, he shook his head. "No way!" Now he's hiking through Glacier National Park lugging sixty-pound packs. I find that hard work, but he's still having fun!

SYNCHRODIVINITY

Everything we need is waiting for us, if we simply take the time to listen to our spirit.

When you start uncovering and rewriting your limiting tribal beliefs, you won't be *thinking over* the question of whether a particular belief is in alignment with your higher self. You'll simply consult your spirit. How? By noticing what's happening in your body. You'll be able to physically *feel* the difference between a belief that's in conflict with your soul and one that's in harmony with it. (More on that later.)

When you're in conflict, your energy sinks. You feel sluggish, tired, perhaps even trapped and resentful. This is a clear indication that your spirit is telling you, NO! However, now your mind will chime in and tell you all the reasons that you *should* be doing what you don't want to do. Once you recognize that this prolonged and onerous debate where you rationalize and defend your position—what I call mental Ping-Pong—is how you ignore your spirit, you can quiet your thoughts. This is when the fear surfaces, and the guilt arrives on cue.

My definition of guilt is quite simple: when you try to force yourself to do something you really don't want to do. It's another way of saying, I'm scared the tribe will be angry with me; I fear for my reputation and standing within the tribe. Anytime you hear yourself say, "I should, I'm supposed to, I have to," you have ignored your spirit to please your tribe.

Coming into harmony with your soul releases the tension in your body and eliminates the mental Ping-Pong. When you hear your spirit, there is a huge surge of energy with a wonderful feeling of relief. Suddenly you are awake, alert, and fully alive and ready to live.

Hope took a large fall in life. She even had to take a sabbatical from her profession because she simply could not face the world. I saw a picture of her hiding under the covers, wishing she could "wake up" from her nightmare. The cause for her fall was immediately evident. I asked her: "*What did you know that you didn't want to know,* just before you dove under the covers?"

Her answer was swift. "I hate my job." Hope had nine more years before retirement and woke up one morning knowing that nine more years would suck the life out of her and that she needed to change jobs. Her spirit had spoken until her mind shushed it with mental Ping-Pong. She was in conflict, because her tribe said *You never leave a good job, but be thankful that you have it.* The stress from breaking a tribal taboo and the thought of nine more years overwhelmed her and caused a terrible depression and lassitude. The conflict sucked the life out of her.

We rewrote her tribal beliefs about her job and she had to make a decision: Was being loyal to her tribe worth the loss of her health and ultimately her life? A true crossroad for her; thankfully, she made some smart choices and is ready and eagerly anticipating her new career.

When I talk about the sinking and surging of your energy, I am not speaking metaphorically. This is literally what happened to Hope. Human beings are composed entirely of energy. Like all living things on our planet, we are a collection of constantly moving molecules, atoms, and subatomic particles. This electromagnetic energy, which is present in every cell in our bodies, is our basic life force. It is what enables CAT scans and MRI scanners to read what is happening inside our bodies.

This electromagnetic energy radiates from our cells in the form of vibrations. Depending on our circumstances, these vibrations can be low to high. When you are healthy, your vibration is high. This is your natural state and a state you can aspire to by doing things that raise your vibration. When you are in a positive frame of mind, are thinking and feeling happy things, or are feeling grateful, your vibration stays high. When you listen to your spirit and end the conflict, your vibration rises.

When your vibration drops, so does the ability of your immune system to fight off illness. When you expect the worst, are reliving past failures in your mind, or are feeling bitter or angry, your vibration drops. Your cells are listening to everything you say and think. What has become clear to me over the years is that toxic thoughts or being around toxic people contaminates the mind and eventually ages and destroys our cells— unless you have no conflict about being toxic. For example, praying for forgiveness from a loving God and then criticizing yourself is a conflict. You recognize that compassion and forgiveness are good qualities and you make the choice to be a better person. For you, being negative is terribly toxic to the body's cells—can you see why it is so important to do an inventory of your limiting tribal beliefs? I see this toxicity in your energy field. Your cells look and feel sick. Adhering to a tribal belief that lowers your vibration is akin to drinking polluted water.

When you focus on your shortcomings or mistakes (*if you forgive yourself too easily, it means you are not a good person—good people feel guilty a long time*), your thoughts are toxic, and toxic thoughts will poison the mind and eventually the body. Being unforgiving or hard on yourself separates you from the love and nurturing of others, even though you need and crave it—that's the conflict. Refusing to forgive yourself for past misdeeds makes it difficult to hear or feel the energy of God or a Higher Power. This negativity and lack of love for yourself drains your life force and diminishes your electromagnetic field. Often with clients who are depressed, their field is muted, gray, and lacking any pizzazz!

This pattern is identical when it comes to your spirit. When you are living in alignment with your soul, your energy vibrates at a very high frequency, but when you ignore your soul, your vibration sinks. Eventually your soul becomes harder to hear—even though that whisper grows to a loud knocking—and with enough hard work, you can blot out your spirit like your energy field. During a Reading I see gray where there was once bright light. There is a lack of hope, an emptiness, and at times, even a darkness of conscience. When babies are born, their spirits are bright and clean and clear. It takes years of struggle to ignore your soul and eventually snuff out its light. It is a sad sight, as often these spiritless people walk the world without care of or compassion for others, and they sometimes do wicked things. Unfortunately, there is no stereotypical look to them—they could be your pharmacist, your neighbor, or a member of your church.

Can you understand why I am so motivated to help you uncover your limiting beliefs and let your spirit soar? Do you understand that you will be leaders of sorts—for your families and friends—because you had the courage to look beyond what appears obvious, and search for more? You had the chutzpah to challenge a way of life that doesn't honor the life you were gifted. You took a risk of hurting a loved one's feelings to follow your truth. Wow! Do I ever salute you and welcome you to the tribe!

I want you to take a look at the following list of some of the tribal beliefs I've heard from people in my workshops. As you read through them, see if any of them seems true to you. If so, you should make a note of it. But before you insist that your tribal belief *is* true, consider the questions that follow each tribal belief.

- Openhearted people are weak.
  Do you know any strong openhearted people? If you get stuck, think about a particular gentle football player or two who come to mind.
- True love only comes around once in life—(subtext: if you are lucky).
  Do you know anyone who is happily married a second time? Do you have any say in opening your heart and falling in love or is it controlled by some unseen forces of the universe?
- Creative people have to suffer to produce great works—just look at Sylvia Plath; she eventually committed suicide.
  Do you know any happy painters or writers?
- You never heal from childhood abuse.
  Do people have any influence in their healing? Is it possible that even something hellacious like childhood abuse can begin to heal by

making a choice to heal, rather than cementing in the idea that healing is impossible?

- Forgiving yourself for a mistake means you don't feel bad that you made it.
  If you can forgive others and still see them as good people, can you choose to forgive yourself—or are you special? And if you can't forgive others, do you think it is a tad prideful to play God?

- Taking care of yourself before others is selfish.
  Is it possible that taking care of yourself first will allow you to take better care of others? Have you ever been cared for or worked with a cranky, tired, resentful sleep-deprived nurse?

- You can't always tell your friends the truth because it will hurt their feelings.
  Is it possible that even though you may initially hurt a friend's feelings by speaking your truth, they will have more respect for you (they will recognize that you took a risk by being authentic because true intimacy is important among friends) and feel safer with you (because they will always know that at least you will tell them the truth—if their butt does look big in those pants!).

- You have to keep the peace at all costs.
  Is it possible that keeping the peace at all costs is dishonest and out of integrity?

- The single most destructive element in life is anger.
  Is anger truly destructive or is it the way in which one expresses it? Can anger be channeled in a healthy way, such as competitive sports or research?

In my workshops, people adamantly insist they do not have such silly and illogical tribal beliefs. However, when I Read them, they reluctantly acknowledge that they do. Having even one of these tribal beliefs can drain your energy and lower your vibration because it can put you into conflict or create tremendous suffering. Think back to a moderate to large mistake you made in your past. Now imagine that you can never forgive yourself for it and that you must always pay a penance for it because you want to be a good person—and good people never let themselves off the hook. For some of you it's very easy to imagine. But I will show you how to change it.

> *When you follow a tribal belief at odds with your spirit, your spiritual energy centers (chakras) begin to shut down.*

By considering alternate possibilities, you have taken the first step toward listening to your spirit: being willing. Each time you are willing and open to new possibilities you can improve your present and future health. *That's why rewriting your tribal beliefs is the very best kind of preventive medicine.*

As your spiritual energy centers begin to shut down, vague and often ignored symptoms such as tiredness, the blues, and minor aches and pains emerge. You pop an aspirin, vow to get more rest, and chalk up your physical complaints to stress. As time goes on, your body speaks more loudly to you. Your symptoms increase in severity or change to ones you find harder to ignore. You notice you have lost the spring in your step. Perhaps you feel a little depressed and occasionally apathetic. Perhaps you get more colds. Events and activities that used to make you smile no longer rouse your excitement. Life has become steady and even-keeled, no major highs and no major lows. Yet.

I want to point out, however, that not all illness is energetically caused. Some people suffer with illnesses caused by poisons in the environment or from genes they have inherited. But when your energy is torn between your loyalty to tribal beliefs that demand you behave one way and your spirit, which yearns for you to do things differently, you get the type of conflict that can bring on disease. This conflict at its worst causes you mental anguish, endless inner debate, guilt, and indecisiveness, all of which wreak havoc with your immune system. This conflict at its best causes resentment, unhappiness, and irritation. As you can see, all conflict lowers your vibration to some degree. You are single-handedly fighting both sides of the battle—the side that wants to follow the tribe and the side that wants to follow your soul.

I see a person's conflicts in specific parts of his or her energy field. If I gave you an energy meter, you would notice a sharp decline of electromagnetic energy represented with colors and waves of energy (similar to shimmering waves of heat rising from the pavement) over the area of the crown of the head and the heart. Additionally, there would be areas of flatness—no palpable or discernible waves of energy emanating from a person—meaning I can only feel tension or tightness; nothing feels smooth or flowing.

Pride will make your search for the divine an intellectual pursuit rather than a heartfelt relationship.

I want to pause here a moment and explain that there are people in the world who live long lives despite having a low vibration. They are critical, negative, narcissistic, abusive, hurtful, and live a life that would be toxic to most human beings, yet it doesn't seem to affect them. The key is the amount of conflict a person is in. If a person feels justified in being hurtful or abusive, or feels okay about lying or cheating, then he or she is not in conflict. Often people like this have muted the voice of their spirit. (In a Reading they are dark, sticky, and dead—there is no high vibration or presence of light or the divine. Vacuous, prideful, and living totally in their heads, they lack humanity as their egos run wild. They need to be in control and can justify every negative or toxic thing they do. Their pride is so great, the divine becomes an intellectual pursuit rather than a heartfelt relationship.) When you meet people like this, you will know because you will feel like you are alone when you are with them, and can't wait to get away from them. I suggest you follow your intuition and run.

If a person is following a limiting tribal belief and doesn't feel any conflict about doing so, he or she is less likely to become ill than people who are following tribal beliefs that no longer fit for them. In other words, the more you are trying to wake up spiritually, the more likely it is you will become ill when you ignore your soul's wake-up calls. Once you know

Truth, you can't ignore it and shove it back into the closet. It's nearly impossible to have an epiphany and then act like someone who is asleep. Talk about a conflict!

This is because it takes a lot of energy to convince ourselves that we are happy when we are not. I watched a recently engaged young woman attempt to convince everyone how delighted she was to be getting married. Her words were empty, however, as her spirit did not support her decision. Instead of feeling energized by her choice, she wondered aloud why her body ached, she was tired all the time, and she had difficulty making decisions. The answer was that all her energy was being used up handling the chaos in her mind, the pain in her heart, her fear of disappointing her family and friends, her anger at feeling trapped, the craziness of feeling good and bad at the same time, and the uncertainty that plagued her every waking moment. Our bodies talk to us all the time, if only we would listen.

I have often asked a client, "How sick do you have to get in order to have permission to leave your business (or profession)?" Or "How stressed or depressed do you have to get?" You see, illness is a socially acceptable reason to do something our tribal beliefs won't allow, like leave a job, a marriage, or other situation that is in conflict with our souls. Unfortunately, even the threat of illness isn't always enough to force people to examine their conflicts. I have watched people die to remain loyal.

Energy invested in a losing battle results in symptoms.

A forty-five-year-old woman became sick with lymphoma after expending too much energy trying to make an abusive marriage work. Her tribal belief that marriage is forever kept her chained to her spouse. "Till death do us part" was taken quite literally. In her Reading I explained that she needed to divorce him and cut the energetic ties to begin her healing. Her siblings had been trying to get her out of the marriage for years.

She reluctantly had her lawyer draw up the divorce papers and bring them to her in her bed. Then she made a crucial decision. She simply could not break her marriage vow, and dying was the only way to end her marriage. She died in bed moments later, papers unsigned, but free of her abusive husband.

Her death was tragic, and unfortunately I've seen similar situations all too often. Are you using illness or burnout in your life to give yourself permission to get out of a certain situation? Wouldn't you rather leave without an illness? You can, by creating a new tribal belief based on the voice of your spirit that is good for you.

Here's the great thing about working with tribal beliefs. They either raise your vibration or not. They are either in alignment with your spirit or not. They are either good for you and make you feel strong, vibrant, and energized, or they do not. There's no in between. *This is one of those areas where the answer to the question Does this raise my vibration? is a clear yes or no.*

There have been many times when someone has told me something that they thought was true ("Sure, I love building the new house . . . Yes, I really do love my husband . . . Of course I'm happy taking care of my neighbor's kids"). But energetically, I can see their energy is dull, ill defined, and lackluster even as they are carrying on about how great their life is. I barely hear those words as I am watching their vibration plummet during their monologue and already know the truth. Eventually their words trail off. They look at me and usually ask sheepishly, "It doesn't raise my vibration, right?" You know the old adage, If you have to ask . . .

Your spirit will never misguide you, lie to you, or point you toward anything but your highest good. Ethereal in nature, your spirit is the bridge between you and God. All of the divine's qualities—endless patience with your resistance and pride; unconditional love for you; total forgiveness; guidance, comfort, strength for the asking; and unwavering support for your growth and happiness—are infused in your spirit. That's why your spirit is tenacious—to help you evolve spiritually and connect more deeply with the divine. Your spirit knows that relationship well and wants you to remember it and embrace it fully.

4.

The Clout of Your Energetic Intentions

YOU HAVE THE LEADING ROLE
IN CREATING YOUR REALITY

Would you want to reinforce to *your* cells that healing is impossible? Or that it takes a long time? On more than one occasion in my healing work, I have been stopped in midsentence by a person who has claimed, "I can't heal from cancer, it's incurable." Can you imagine the impact of that tribal belief on that individual's chemotherapy or radiation regimen? Would you want to lock in your fate with a negative outcome? Or would you consider giving yourself a chance at a different outcome by being open to a different possibility than the one you so steadfastly and reverently defend?

Even if all you did was rewrite your tribal belief to *It is reasonable to believe that I might recover from this illness,* it would make a huge difference energetically. You have the power to set whatever energetic intention you choose. Remember, your spirit has a whole list of tribal beliefs that are good for you!

When I do a Reading on someone, I can see the person's illness (or future susceptibility to a particular illness) based on the vibration of the molecules in his or her body. Each disease has its own unique vibration. I learned this during my years as an ER nurse, when my intuitive diagnoses were confirmed time and again by the results of a patient's lab test. I have also learned in my years as a Medical Intuitive that certain tribal beliefs are associated with certain diseases. For example, the vibration of fibromyalgia, chronic fatigue, and lupus are extremely similar at the first level of the Reading. In people with these illnesses, I usually find an inability to enjoy life. People's reasons for not enjoying life may differ (*Life is a serious business—If I'm too happy nothing will get accomplished;* or *I made a big mistake earlier in life and shouldn't be allowed to enjoy my life*—another way of saying *I don't deserve to be happy*), but their main energetic focus is that they don't enjoy life. As I Read a person's energy field more in-depth, the energetic signature for the illness becomes more focused and the particular beliefs more exact and pronounced.

Please note that it was not their illness that initially prevented them from enjoying life. It was their tribal belief. This belief has been with them since childhood, and it opened them to the disease long before they actually became sick. Of course, the debilitating nature of these illnesses reinforces the person's belief that life is not meant to be enjoyed! And eventually, the illness itself actually prevents people from enjoying life. Their tribal belief has become a reality. This is not unusual. You might call it a self-fulfilling prophecy. I call it the result of setting an energetic intention.

Let me explain. We've all heard that a positive attitude is important. The reason this is true is because of the effect positive thoughts have on your energy. Besides raising your vibration and making you feel better, thinking positively sets an intention that will powerfully affect the life you create for yourself. However, simply slathering positive thoughts around a limiting tribal belief will not raise your vibration or change your energetic blueprint. For example, saying a positive affirmation like "I am a channel of life through which the universal creative force finds expression" will do nothing, because it makes no sense. Let me say it differently: What does it look like? How can you create something that you can't define? What exactly does "finds expression" mean? Will you paint, sing, or be of service in the world? Then say so.

Affirmations like "I deserve love and always expect the best" may be in conflict with tribal beliefs that say *You are not lovable unless you serve others,* and *Be careful because the rug can be pulled out at any time.* These beliefs are so powerful they will neutralize such creative and wondrous thoughts. Please heed my advice and work on rewriting your tribals and *then* see how well your affirmations work. You will be thrilled at the results.

Limiting tribal beliefs can nullify your positive affirmations.

Further, a limiting tribal belief can actually breed negative thinking! Consider the limiting belief *Struggle is a way of life, and you should simply buck up and deal with it.* You will awaken each day expecting struggle, and thus not make choices that could end your struggling.

Caitlin came to me feeling trapped and resigned to an unhappy and difficult life. She only came because a friend gifted her a session with me. Caitlin believed she had no power and could make no choices to change her life. Her life, according to her tribe, was already scripted for struggle, and she learned to accept it. Speaking with her was like conversing with Eyore. Their energies matched perfectly. "Poor me (read it with Eyore's heavy, slow, sad, voice), I'll never be happy or find someone special to share my life with. My life is hard, but I try to make the best of it." (She actually told this to people when she first met them.) People fled from her negativity, but she wouldn't acknowledge that she had played a role in her aloneness.

Caitlin had no desire to change. She had no willingness to explore her tribal beliefs and secretly enjoyed her constant struggles, exacerbated by her negative thinking. Her beliefs literally taught her to be negative and expect the worst, and her energy and her life circumstances reflected this. Since she lacked any desire to consider an alternate reality, her Reading was brief.

Jolene had a terrible environmental illness. She became sick around power lines, computers, paints, mold, and even people. All the specialists she consulted said it was incurable, and she would have to suffer from it for her entire life. They gave Jolene books on the subject to educate herself on living with her disease (meaning she would live a lifetime of horror. It was the one and only time I have advocated burning a book!). Jolene felt she had no choice but to believe her doctors because they were the authority. She was resigned to her suffering and found it difficult to look forward to the rest of her life, alone, unable to go outside and participate in normal life.

When she consulted me, I told her that the more she broadcast her belief that her illness was not curable, the stronger it would take hold of her body. I asked if she would simply consider the possibility that she could recover, rather than saying her illness was forever and locking that message into her cells. Next I asked her to rewrite her tribal belief: *Never challenge an authority, especially physicians.* I encouraged her to think outside the box of conventional Western medicine, and asked, "Is it reasonable to believe that healing *might* occur?" She found she could agree with that, even though it was highly unlikely. The next step was to get away from all the friends and family who supported the old belief and to find a new doctor.

Once she got away from the naysayers and began to broadcast the energy of possible healing, things began to change. With each alleviation of her symptoms, she was like a child seeing snow for the first time. In awe, reverence, and disbelief, she continued her healing regimen. Other tribal beliefs such as *Healing is hard* and *Healing takes a long time* slowed her healing process, but nonetheless, she healed! She now uses a computer, talks on the telephone, has picked up her brushes and begun her beloved painting again, and has an active social life. Next month, she's flying to Arizona to hike the Grand Canyon!

Limiting beliefs are like old coats of paint covering your soul; strip them off and let your natural beauty shine.

Your energetic intention also sends a message to the people around you. I call this kind of message an energetic broadcast and it tells people how you wish them to treat you. When I Read people, it's like they are wearing a blaring neon sign on their foreheads. Without opening their mouths, they can teach a room full of people how to treat them.

> *Your energetic broadcast teaches people how to treat you.*

Your energetic broadcast also plays a major role in creating your reality. In the eighteenth century, James Allen caused a stir in writing *As a Man Thinketh*, which explored the power of one's thoughts to create an outcome. He said that circumstances don't make the man, but rather man makes his own circumstances. This dynamic thinker understood our inherent power to shape our lives based on our thoughts and beliefs. Remember that your energetic broadcast is predominantly colored by your limiting beliefs. Change your beliefs, change your broadcast.

Here's how it works. Your broadcast that "hard work is essential for a good character" is an energetic intention that will attract evidence, people, and events to support it. When you take a mental health or play day away from the office, you will feel guilty and energetically apologize for your behavior. This apology will invite judgment and criticism from your boss and colleagues. Their reaction reinforces your belief that people of good character don't goof off.

> *Apology on the inside invites criticism and judgment on the outside.*

It's the same for people who energetically apologize for being gay, rich, powerful, successful, or having ease in life. Remember: an energetic apology on the inside invites criticism and judgment on the outside. If you are feeling judged by others, please check for any apology energy you may be broadcasting. Then, find and rewrite the tribal belief that caused you to apologize in the first place!

Ashley says she wants to be in a relationship quite badly, but her broadcast says, "My needs are not as important as yours." Ashley's message tells people how to treat her—and they do exactly what she broadcasts. They use her.

Because of her broadcast, Ashley attracted people into her life who treated her as unimportant and unlovable; she was unconsciously creating the evidence to support her belief. Ashley ended up surrounded by people who treated her like a doormat and at times bordered on abusive.

When Ashley changed her tribal belief to *It's reasonable to believe that I will speak up for myself on occasion,* it changed her broadcast and the way she responded to people. When her new tribal belief is in complete alignment with her spirit, it will change the type of person she energetically attracts.

Don't kid yourself. Everyone senses energy on some level, whether it be subconscious or not. We are all picking up your broadcast. When it says "I'm worthless," and you broadcast doormat energy to the world, you are inviting people to wipe their feet on you. When your energy says "Don't frighten me," most people will cease to be authentic around you and treat you with kid gloves. If your energy says "The world is not a safe place," you will attract people and events to support your belief.

Even the most accomplished attorneys, CEOs, and musicians—people who appear to be at the top of their game—have personal broadcasts that are influenced by toxic tribal beliefs. An actor I know who plays confident and happy guys actually broadcasts fear of the world and low self-esteem. His personal life is the polar opposite of the confident roles he tries to portray. Thus, his acting is not the best it could be. This incongruence is why you sometimes feel let down after a movie that should have been good. The casting director did not match the person's energetic broadcast to the part.

Remember, we all are capable of reading other people's energy to at least some extent. Pay attention the next time someone's words or actions don't seem to jibe with reality. You are probably reading their energetic broadcast!

The bottom line is this: your broadcast shapes your world, and your tribal beliefs shape your broadcast. Here's how it all fits together. Unless interrupted, this is the progression that stems from ignoring your soul:

Loyalty to a limiting tribal belief
causes conflict with your soul

•

Conflict causes energy drains

•

Energy drains lower your vibration

•

Lowered vibration suppresses the immune system

•

Symptoms, depression, or possible illness

Remember that most people sense your energetic broadcast on some level. If you are trying to follow a limiting belief that is causing internal conflict, your unrest and unhappiness will be apparent to others. This low-vibration state now becomes the essence, or predominant energy, that others note in your broadcast, which can actually repel other people or, at the very least, keep them at a distance.

A classic example is if you have a limiting belief *Don't get too close to people—they will always hurt you.* This belief is in conflict with your need for companionship and will cause a mixed message to others. Your broadcast will tell them you want to be friends, but just as they get close, you will pull away. This dual message is very unsettling to others, especially to children.

So, if your vibration is low—if you aren't happy, if you are ill, or if you are feeling conflicted, guilty, or trapped in any area of your life—please consider the strong possibility that you are living by a tribal belief that is in opposition to what your spirit wants. Dig deep, find the belief, and change it. You will see your vibration rise, your energy increase, and your light shine brighter. You will also find that more people will want to be around you.

We are all naturally drawn to high-vibration people. They're fun to be around and make us feel good. And if we let them, they can help raise our vibration, too—courage, happiness, and commitment to one's soul are contagious!

5.

When Is a "Fact" Not a Fact?

MAKE YOUR OWN HISTORY

Now you understand that your thoughts can lead to mind-body-spirit illness. But how do you know which thoughts are causing your migraines, depression, or fatigue? We've looked at the two influences on your belief system: your tribe and your soul. Now there's just a little more background you need before you start to uncover the tribal beliefs that are driving your life off track.

One of the sneakiest things about tribal beliefs is that we often think they are facts. Here are some tribal beliefs that once passed themselves off as scientific truth.

- The sun revolves around the earth.
- The world is flat.
- Women can't be surgeons because they don't have the fine motor control needed to execute small, precise movements.

All of these "facts" have fallen before the advance of scientific knowledge. As you unveil your own tribal beliefs, you will find many of them falling before the advance of soul's desire for you. And the beliefs you thought were facts will fall with the loudest thud!

Some beliefs are instilled in us with such an air of authority or emphasis that we take them as gospel. "You'll make a lousy wife," your harried mother shouts one morning when she finds dried egg on the plate you washed. "Life is hard," your father tells you with despair in his voice the night he gets laid off. "No pain, no gain!" your coach roars again and again. "You can't have it all," your math teacher declares when you want to reschedule your tutoring sessions so you can try out for the school play.

When a tribal belief is spoken aloud in my workshops, I watch the room react: those who wholeheartedly agree and think the belief is fact, those who simply shake their heads in disbelief, and those who shake their heads only to discover later that they do have that belief. Be aware of the silent yet powerful subtext that follows each belief.

Here are a few of these beliefs:

- God is vengeful and waiting for me to make a mistake and wants me to suffer.

- Some mistakes are not forgivable (including premarital sex, abortion, and cheating on your spouse).
- When I've made a terrible decision with terrible repercussions, I have to pay for it my entire life. I can never forget it or it will show that I am not an ethical or good person.
- I can't go skiing for Thanksgiving or Christmas—it's a time for family.
- I can't tell my friend that her whining is driving me crazy. That would be rude and might hurt her feelings.
- You have to be very patient and nice to sick people.

Now, to illustrate the difference, here are a few facts:

- The sun rises in the east.
- Men have one X and one Y chromosome.
- Diamonds are so hard they can cut glass.

A fact, according to the *Compact Oxford English Dictionary,* is "a thing that is indisputably the case." As another dictionary puts it, a fact is "truth or reality, as distinct from mere statement or belief." In other words, if you can put the words "I think" in front of a statement, it's a belief. For example, "I think you have to be very patient and nice to sick people." Or "I think some mistakes are not forgivable." Fine. Those are clearly beliefs then, not facts. When you put "I think" in front of a genuine fact, it makes nonsense of it (or of you): "I think the sun rises in the east"; "I think diamonds are so hard they cut glass."

So don't let tribal beliefs fool you into thinking they are

facts. If they are not indisputable, they are just beliefs. They don't deserve your undying homage—especially if they're killing off your health and happiness.

Friends Don't Let Friends Drive Unconsciously

Many limiting tribal beliefs live in your unconscious mind. You do not know they exist. In fact, you often think that you believe just the opposite. In my work I am constantly amazed at the discrepancy between what most people think they believe and the beliefs in their energy system that they actually live by.

Often people claim to disagree with a tribal belief, but I see that they energetically fully believe it. This is exactly what an unconscious driver is: a belief that controls our behavior, choices, feelings, and perceptions that we are completely unaware of. Unaware means you operate without choices, blindly and obediently following an old way of life whether it is good for you or not!

I have watched people completely skip over identifying a belief and, instead, ascribe their choices to something else entirely. One woman told me that she stayed in an unhappy and emotionally abusive relationship for several months because "I wanted to be loved so badly."

"No," I replied. "It's your tribal belief that *Love requires sacrifice.*"

Shocked at first, she told me that seemed true, like a fact, and could actually trace that need for sacrifice in all of her relationships.

Had this women been in therapy, she no doubt would have been guided to analyze her neediness, her habit of sharing too much too fast early in a relationship, and her need to recognize emotional abuse. This saddens me because all this woman needs to do is change her tribal belief about love requiring sacrifice, and these other problems would clear up.

I am still to this day amazed at the complexity of human problems and suffering that can be cleared up and resolved completely by changing one tribal belief. Please realize that limiting tribal beliefs about love, for example, can relate to all relationships—siblings, friends, parents.

Limiting beliefs about love will instigate difficulties in all of your relationships.

Tricia came to me with long-standing depression and anxiety, not helped by her antidepressants. Her unhappiness was palpable as was her tribal belief that was causing many of her problems. When I looked in the area of her energy field where I see the quality of a person's relationship with their family of origin (the bottom of the torso), I saw nothing and felt nothing, as though she had no parents but had been raised by wolves.

Her mother, a dramatic and manipulative woman, had not instilled any level of safety, love, or trust in their relationship. In fact, she was demanding, attention seeking, and derogatory to Tricia, often pointing out what a poor excuse for a daughter she was. Tricia literally sacrificed her own emotional happiness, bending into an energetic pretzel, to appease her mother during her frequent and extended visits. When I asked why, she replied: *"Because that's the nature of love. When you love someone, you give up everything for them."*

I pointed out how that tribal belief had ruled every loving relationship Tricia ever had. She soon began to point out specific behaviors that were a direct result of her low-vibration belief. She rewrote her beliefs about love, her depression is all but gone, and her mother rarely visits anymore!

Brian is miserable—and he's in quite a predicament. He wants to get close to people but feels trapped when he begins to love or care for anyone. He came to me because he was tired of the internal battle.

"I don't understand," he began. "It makes sense to get close to people, yet each time I begin a new friendship or relationship, I do something to destroy it. I'm left feeling bad and good at the same time. For some odd reason, I feel like running the minute I get close to people. It feels suffocating. I've analyzed the situation and simply can't figure out my problem."

Brian thought he needed to stay loyal to two opposing ideas—both of which had supporting evidence: *Love is painful and should be avoided at all costs*—he learned this from his mother, and *Love is wonderful*—he learned this from literature.

Can you see the conflict that he was in? While his education about love was on opposite ends of the spectrum, his real problem was his black and white thinking. The actual tribal belief causing his distress was *People are either good or bad*—a powerful message from his mother, who had never forgiven herself for being a single, unwed mother.

When I asked him if people could be all good or all bad, he said no. Like most people, Brian was following a tribal belief unconsciously. Once he recognized this, we rewrote the tribal belief together and began to heal his spirit by taking him out of conflict, giving his spirit a voice, and teaching him to recognize it! He is now in a very close and loving relationship with a wonderful woman.

One way to uncover your unconscious beliefs is to ask your siblings what they learned about life. Chances are, you learned the same thing. Tell your belief to a friend and listen closely to the response. Do you get an affirming nod, or a blank stare of disbelief? The wider and more diverse your circle of friends, the more varied the beliefs—but what someone says is a fact may be challenged by the way he or she lives life.

For example, do your friends complain about a lack of free time because they work so much—because it's the only way to get ahead and make money? When studying for finals do your friends insist on studying every night—long and laboriously—because that's the only way to pass their tests? What do they think about the person who is plunked in front of the TV instead?

Examining, questioning, and revamping some of the rules that govern your life will change your unconscious behaviors into conscious choices. These choices can set you free from the bondage of suffering, hard work, and denial and lead you to a life of abundance, joy, and spontaneity.

- Imagine if you could love freely without the resentment or fear of having to sacrifice throughout the relationship.
- Imagine trusting your intuition that you can relax because you are ready for your exam even though you still have three days to study.
- Imagine if you could breathe fully and deeply without the suffocating restraints of following someone else's prescription for life, and followed the voice of your spirit.

Dare to think outside the tribe and question what appears to be a fact. And when your various tribes look askance at your new behavior, consider sharing your newfound insights with them. You wouldn't let a friend drive while he's drunk—why let a friend be a slave to a set of rules based on scarcity, fear, or ignorance?

Jill is a gentle forty-five-year-old professional who works very hard and is very successful. Her list of accomplishments is quite long. She takes care of herself—or so she claims—until it comes to her father. He is a diagnosed narcissist who can only engage with his daughter if he is benefiting from the engagement. That might mean attention and sympathy for him, a moment of power wielded over her, or the sheer delight of pointing out that his needs are far more important than hers. He does not give Jill emotional support, but sucks it from her. He doesn't give and take in a conversation; he can only take. And he has never spoken the words Jill has longed to hear for her whole life: "I'm proud of you." Even when she has come right out and asked him if he was proud, he ignores her. He berates her and consistently reminds her that she is a failure for not marrying, so he can never celebrate her accomplishments because they mean nothing to him.

Every time Jill speaks with her father, she feels drained and resentful. This had gotten to the point where she was getting repeated colds. When I asked her why she spoke to him so much if it made her sick, she said, "Because he is my father."

That didn't quite answer my question and so I persisted. "What if he were a coworker who drained you so much? Would you continue to talk to him?"

"Absolutely not," she exclaimed emphatically.

"Okay, what if he were a friend who drained you so much—would you continue to talk to him?"

"Probably not," she replied.

"And why is that?"

"Because he would only be a friend, not a parent."

"So a parent has the right to make you feel so miserable about yourself, and you have the duty to take your punishment?"

She stopped cold and I knew I had opened the door for her spirit to heal. I heard the sound of freedom ringing in her heart as she broke down in tears.

"No, that doesn't seem quite right," she said quietly.

This was a moment for celebration. She had stopped to consider a life based on rote and rules and begun to consider what was healing for her spirit.

Now I asked Jill to examine the *unconscious tribal belief* that had been ruling her life: *Honor thy father—no matter what.* Jill knew she felt drained after her conversations with her father, knew she didn't look forward to speaking with him, and knew (on some level) that she would never win his approval. But she was not aware that her tribal belief forced her to return to him for more punishment.

Unconscious beliefs like this are part of your energetic blueprint; I can see them, but you generally can't see them on your own. Or you may have been aware of them at one point, but now have forgotten them. Unfortunately, you still live by them. These beliefs have silenced your spirit's voice and begun to thwart your best efforts to be true to yourself. This is what I call living according to the mind's rules rather than the soul's rules. When this happens, the body is caught in the middle and bears the brunt of the disagreement.

Jill's body always got weak after talking to her father; her immune system always lost some of its ability to protect her. That's why she always ended up with a cold. Family holidays were the worst. The prolonged exposure to such a toxic human being left her recuperating in bed for days after the holiday.

It's important to note that Jill did not get sick from being around a toxic human being. She got sick from the conflict inside her between following her tribal belief that she must honor her father (by visiting and talking with him) and her soul's desire that she honor and protect herself (by staying away from him and avoiding his emotional abuse).

Jill needed to answer a few questions with total honesty before she could resolve her relationship with her father.

- Was she supporting her spirit when she repeatedly accepted such denigration?
- Was she giving her power away to her father simply because she shared the same blood type or he is older, or an authority figure?
- Was she being authentic and honest, and speaking up for herself?
- Was she prostituting herself for a secondary gain such as love or approval?

Jill now recognized that she was not honoring herself. She rewrote her tribal belief to *It is reasonable to believe that I can honor my father without sacrificing myself.* First, she told her father that his words were hurtful, but was met with a blank stare. Next she asked for respect, but her father seemed unable to comply with or simply ignored her request. Third she chose to seek approval elsewhere—from herself, her coworkers, and her friends.

Now it was time to change her unconscious habits. She replaced many personal visits with brief telephone calls. When interacting with her father, she continually asked herself if the conversation supported her spirit—raised her vibration—or not. Each time she answered this question, she had a *conscious choice to take care of herself, or be ill.*

Jill used different techniques to take care of herself. She would get off the telephone and go for a walk, limit the interaction, or end the conversation. Jill now understood there was no law saying she had to tolerate such toxic behavior. Next she prayed for him, sending him healing white light and the best energy she could conjure. Jill understood that she didn't have to stop loving him, but she also didn't have to force herself to be with someone she disliked. She was no longer drained or resentful because she focused on respecting herself and others. Her new choices, boundaries, and energetic broadcast began to reshape her relationship in a positive way.

At the start of Jill's story I mentioned that she felt she took good care of herself. Yet allowing someone to spew toxic words at you is akin to swimming in the Ganges River in India. Although it is one of the most polluted rivers in the world, millions go to the Ganges each year on pilgrimage to take a ritual bath in its sacred waters. I once asked a pilgrim, "If you were not on a spiritual journey, would you immerse yourself in a polluted river?"

"No way!" he replied. "That's disgusting. You could get very sick. But *this* is the Ganges!"

That's the power of an unconscious tribal belief—you will immerse yourself in toxic situations because you are supposed to. Trust me when I say, if you had consulted your soul, you would not dip a toe in the Ganges!

So how do smart people like Tricia, Brian, and Jill get caught in such conflict? It's because so many tribal beliefs are simply not on the conscious playing field. They belong to:

- The part of you that you are not fully conscious or aware of, also known as your energetic blueprint— a myriad of information from your past, your patterns, your archetypal makeup, your fears, and your wounds.
- The part of you that wants to fit in and be accepted by your various tribes by following their rules. This part says *It is more important to be accepted by the tribe than to be true to myself.*
- The part of you that *chooses* to operate without consulting your spirit or guidance first.

The more you read, the more conscious you become and the faster you can change your life for the better. The only thing that would slow you down is a belief that says *Change takes a long time.*

Showstopper Beliefs

Even when people become aware they are living their lives according to tribal beliefs—beliefs they *know* aren't good for them—they often think they don't have a choice. Well, I am asking you to consider several truths that will stir, excite, and change your life for the better:

- The laws you have lived by may not be in alignment with your spirit.

- Life is easier when you live in agreement with your spirit.
- You can create a better reality both easily and quickly.

Did that last one give you pause?

Before we go any further, we need to look at what I call showstopper beliefs. These are tribal beliefs that will prevent you from changing any of your other tribal beliefs. Let's take a look.

Three beliefs—*Change is hard, Change takes a long time,* and *I have no choice*—will prove themselves true if you are attached to them. As you begin your journey of transforming your life, please consider rewriting these three beliefs before any other. I have done many Readings on people who could have healed a myriad of mind-body-spirit illnesses easily and quickly but refused to entertain the possibility that their reality was wrong. They pursued long, arduously complicated and expensive healing regimens without success and returned to me wondering why.

I've said it so many times: the Read is the Read, and it doesn't change because you don't like it. Until you rewrite those beliefs, they will stand in your way and control your healing. If you believe that you must work hard to change—that it takes a long time, perhaps causes a few sleepless nights, and certainly must disrupt your daily routine, that reality will come to pass. I don't like to watch people struggle and suffer needlessly. When I find someone trying to heal an issue with the belief *Change is hard,* I try to make it hard for them by having them rewrite tribal beliefs while standing on one foot and hopping up and down with their eyes closed!

CHANGE

*Your energetic broadcast will create the evidence needed to
support your beliefs and make them a reality.*

If you think any of these things are true, you are going
to have a very hard time changing any of your other tribal
beliefs, no matter how much you want to. Let me show you
a couple of quick ways to find some alternatives to them.
Oops, I challenged your limiting belief by implying it could
be easy.

Let's say you believe *Change is hard.* In certain situations that's
been your experience, right? (We'll ignore the fact for now that
you have been sending energetic broadcasts to this effect, thus
fulfilling your own prophecy.) Has this been your experience
100 percent of the time? Can you think of a single time in your
life when change was not hard? It could have been a small
change. Any change at all.

I have watched so many people instantly change a limiting
belief simply by having the awareness and the willingness to
consider different possibilities from what they tenaciously adhere to. For example, I asked Hannah, who was rather afraid of
God and therefore rarely asked for help, to ask for help and
consolation during a stressful time. Immediately she gave me
five reasons why it would be hard to ask; she was beginning to
create a reality where it was hard to ask God for help. I said,
"For the moment, ignore your reasons and just do it."

Hannah made a life-changing choice that afternoon and

asked God for comfort and help. Guided to take a walk during her lunch break, she came across a small church that she had never seen before and decided to look inside. There on the door, etched in the glass, was the word *Hannah.* Her fears were replaced by laughter and a sudden rush of warmth and comfort as she went in to continue her chat with the divine. She learned that the doors had been donated in honor of Hannah, mother of one of the parishioners. Hannah experienced a moment of synchrodivinity—because she was willing to take a risk and look beyond her limiting beliefs that change had to be hard.

I bet you can think of something, because it is not a law of the universe that change is hard. Okay, are you willing to consider that not all change is hard? "Yes," you say, "but you're just talking about small changes. All big changes are hard." Are they? Did you ever get an offer of a job that you weren't expecting— or know anyone who did? Did you ever fall in love easily—or know anyone who did? Did you ever see something or go somewhere and suddenly say, "I have to have that," or "I have to do that," or "I have to live there," and you made it happen? Or do you know anyone who did? The answer has to be yes. So there goes *Change is hard.* It's an overstatement. How about considering *It's reasonable to believe that not all change has to be hard*—at least until you learn how to rewrite that one in your own words, according to the guidance of your soul.

Now that you've considered the possibility that change isn't hard, how long must it take? Does it really take a long time, or are you making it take a long time? Do you have to consider, and think, and rationalize, and explore the pros and cons, or can you, like Hannah, just do it—now.

On to the final entrant in our trio of "when your reality isn't right" tribal beliefs: *I have no choice.*

- They are my family and I have no choice but to love them.
- Two doctors say I'm terminal. I have no choice but to believe them.
- I was abused as a child and have no choice but to be damaged for life.

Fortunately, *I have no choice* quickly turns into *I didn't know I had a choice.* There is a poignant scene in the movie *Gladiator* with Russell Crowe about choice. He is enslaved and forced to fight to the death as a gladiator. Suddenly, he has a moment of inspiration that changes his entire energetic blueprint. He decides not to go into the arena and fight. His master tells him, "Then you will die." The unspoken agreement is, "Then so be it."

The point is that the gladiator recognized that he was not trapped—he was still a man capable of choices. While it's true that both choices—to fight or not—would lead to his death, he had a say in his destiny. In that moment, he was no longer a slave, but a free man. I am asking you to experience one of those poignant moments now—to recognize that you do have choices, and you do play a significant role in the reality you create for yourself.

So can we agree that for now you will (provisionally) believe the following?

- Change doesn't always have to be hard.
- Change doesn't always take a long time.
- Having a choice is part of what makes us human.

Great! Now the show can go on.

Five Stages of Changing a Tribal Belief

We depend on our tribal beliefs to protect and guide us, so naturally we react with shock and disbelief when we first learn that a tribal belief may neither be true nor good guidance for leading a wonderful life. This is similar to the first stage of Elisabeth Kübler-Ross's five stages of grief. People go through these five stages when learning of a terminal illness or experiencing a death or some other significant loss in their lives.

Uncovering a false tribal belief definitely qualifies as a significant loss, and I have watched clients go through these same five stages. For some it happens in a matter of minutes, for others it takes years.

I. Shock and Denial ("What do you mean by saying struggle doesn't build character? Of course it does!" And then: "I couldn't have this belief—it's dumb!")

2. Anger ("What was my family thinking when they taught me this nonsense?" "Why did my choir teacher tell me I couldn't sing?")

3. Bargaining or Negotiation ("Well, I could change it a little bit." "Maybe I can change my tribal beliefs about my friends, but I'm not going to rock the boat with my family.")

4. Depression ("What have I done? I've wasted so many years being loyal to this tribal belief and it's all been a stupid mistake.")

5. Acceptance or Willingness ("Okay, I see that these beliefs are not in my highest good and I'm ready to start changing them.")

Just like when you've lost a loved one, your good health depends on going through all five stages. When a tribal belief is at odds with your spirit and you stall in any stage, your energy begins to evaporate. The negotiation stage can consume you for days, weeks, or even years. The more time you spend bargaining, the greater your loss of emotional, spiritual, and physical energy—and the more severe your eventual diagnosis.

Taught as a child *Struggle builds character,* Maureen welcomed her life challenges as opportunities to become a better person. Nested within this belief was yet another tribal belief, which decreed *Asking for help is the sign of a weak person—or one of little character.*

She came to see me because she felt exhausted, trapped, and without hope. She reminded me of Sisyphus. The gods had condemned Sisyphus to ceaselessly rolling a rock to the top of a mountain, only to have the stone roll back down the hill. Repeatedly, he pushed a heavy boulder uphill, only to fail at his endeavor.

When I first approached Maureen about considering the possibility that her life could be different if she got some help with the things she was struggling with, she was adamant.

"I am a better person for my struggles," she declared, "and I take pride in overcoming them on my own. I am not a weak person—I rarely if ever ask for help."

Maureen was clearly in shock that I would suggest something contrary to her belief. I knew I was on dangerous ground—challenging her family's beliefs was tantamount to blasphemy, and we all know what happens when you challenge someone's family! I asked Maureen to consider the possibility that asking for help does not show weakness in a person, it just makes their life easier, and it's okay for life to be easy.

She bristled and launched into a tirade about how life was fraught with struggle and, consequently, it was not and could not be easy. She ended with a firm statement of "fact": "I can only depend on myself, and if I don't learn to be strong, I will be in big trouble when life throws me a curveball."

I ended our session asking her to ponder one of my favorite sayings: "The true measure of a person's strength is their ability to be vulnerable."

A month later, Maureen lost her job and told no one. By the time I heard about it, she was eating canned soup and crackers for her meals and had almost lost her house. It took her nine months to recover from the financial crisis.

The next time Maureen came to a workshop, I approached her beliefs from a logical instead of an emotional viewpoint—I left her tribe out of the discussion. I mentioned that recently I had been driving to a cabin high in the mountains and encountered a tree across the road. I had to choose whether to try to move it on my own or ask some neighbors down the road for help. She nodded when I told her I asked for help.

"Well, of course," she commented. "It would have been stupid to move the tree on your own when the farmers made it an easier job."

I agreed with her and then asked the big question: "Do you think I'm a weak person for asking for help?"

Maureen sputtered and opened her mouth to make a sarcastic reply but nothing came out. I smiled and waited. I knew a great "Aha!" was coming. Like Sisyphus, Maureen was beginning to realize there was no more dreadful punishment than futile and hopeless labor—and it wasn't building her character! She had identified a tribal belief that caused her to make decisions that were not in her highest good. She had logically deduced that her family might have been in error. She was shocked and dumbstruck.

Maureen did not stop there, however. Her epiphany followed the five stages. Her next reaction was anger. "What were my parents thinking?" she demanded. "How dare my family teach me such nonsense?"

Her anger evaporated as quickly as it had come as her bond with her tribe took over again. She had entered the third stage:

bargaining, or what I call "the negotiation stage." This is the point where Maureen had to face her conflict: be loyal to tribal law or listen to her spirit. She was nervous about going against her tribe and feared their criticism. The negotiation stage can be filled with emotional turmoil and mental Ping-Pong. Maureen defended and debated the issue back and forth nearly to the point of exhaustion. She said things like, "Well, it is true that we learn something after overcoming a trial. We learn about our strengths and that is part of our character." I let her ramble on. She had held this tribal belief for fifty years; she needed to work it through at her own pace.

As her explanations and rationalizations of her position began to subside, I could read the sadness in her. She was thinking about her past and realizing how many times she had suffered silently and alone. She saw how many times she had inadvertently made life much harder than it needed to be, and all because her tribe had taught her to admire struggle.

As she relived her past, the fourth stage, depression, struck.

"How much time I wasted trying to do things on my own," she lamented. "And what a jerk I have been. I have great friends who wanted to help and I shut them out," she said quietly.

It is this fourth stage where a critical choice is made: to stay there and rehash and lament one's past, to become self-critical or judgmental, or to move on by choosing to rewrite the tribal belief and start your life anew. Maureen stayed in the fourth stage for almost six weeks. She despaired over her past choices, not realizing this was yet another form of struggling to build her character.

Eventually she reached the fifth stage: acceptance. She now faced the truth:

- Although her family meant well, this particular inherited tribal belief was not in her highest good.
- Although she had made her past harder than it needed to be, she could let it go and be in the present with new choices.
- She was responsible for the life she had created, and she *had the power* to change the present and redesign her future, making both much easier.
- She gave herself permission to be disloyal to the old tribal law, and she rewrote her tribal belief to be in alignment with her spirit.
- She celebrated her new tribal belief and welcomed the ease and flow of her new way of living.

The five stages of identifying a tribal belief do not always take so long. I have seen people change tribal beliefs in an instant. One time I saw an amazing transformation happen overnight. A woman I know had to put her beloved eighteen-year-old cat, Ketsie, to sleep. She felt devastated. Her pain was almost unbearable. She prayed that evening for help in dealing with her terrible feelings of grief and loss. In the middle of the night, she awoke with a great Aha! about a tribal belief she had: *Grief is homage.* Being in deep pain about Ketsie's death had been a way to prove her love and show how much she missed her little Ketsie. She realized she could pay homage to him in many other ways. Her grief instantly lifted.

Does she still miss him? Of course. But that dark and devastating grief stopped plaguing her that night and never returned. It was an answer to her prayer.

Here are some keys points to remember as you begin to explore your tribal history and create a new life for yourself:

- Be compassionate with yourself. Uncovering "facts" that are not facts but have been the guiding compass for your life can be both upsetting and exhilarating. At times, it will leave you like a doe in the headlights: knowing you have to move forward on your path, but being mesmerized and nervous to take the first step.

- Your Aha! moment of awareness will at times shock you, but remember—everyone goes through those five stages—it is the natural process of making a sacred choice.

- It is solely your choice how long you park in the third stage, bargaining. The length of time you continue to negotiate will determine the duration and intensity of the amount of struggle you encounter.

- Lingering in the fourth stage, depression, is a waste of your valuable time. You can lament your past or live today and create a wonderful future.

- Just one showstopping belief will do just that—ruin the best show of your life—the one about your happiness, ease, success, and abundance. If you don't remember Hannah, you certainly are familiar with Nike. Rewrite those showstoppers today: just do it!

In the next chapter I'm going to show you how to easily and quickly find the limiting beliefs that are unconsciously ruling your life. I'll show you the impact of a low-vibration belief— I'll help you to diagnose what's wrong with your life and how to fix it. Because if you are anything less than passionate and ecstatic about your life, it's time to get in touch with your spirit and make a sacred choice.

6.

What's in Your Tribal Wallet?

DIAGNOSE WHAT'S NOT WORKING
IN YOUR LIFE

One of the most powerful things you have begun to learn is that you not only play a role in some of the bad things that happen to you, *but* you have the power to change that role. It begins with identifying and rewriting your tribal beliefs, which is one of the most important, liberating, and healing things you will ever do. It is free, quick, and it doesn't require you to take a trip to India. I can guarantee it will begin a profound healing of your spirit. Here are some simple techniques to discover your tribal beliefs.

*Saying "I should," "I'm supposed to," or "I must" before an
action means you aren't doing it because you want to or
choose to.*

Since uncovering tribal beliefs always starts with willingness, begin by asking yourself a few questions:

- Are there ways in which you are giving up your energy, your happiness, and your health for the sake of
  your tribal beliefs?
- Are you content to live the life someone else wants
  you to live—or do you want to explore one beneficial
  and unique to you?
- Are you courageous enough to question the ways you
  were taught in order to find what breathes life into
  your spirit?

A great deal of depression and anxiety is caused by limiting
beliefs that leave you feeling trapped, indecisive, or feeling
guilty for your natural inclinations. Have you ever wanted to
burst into song because you felt happy, or applaud in church because the sermon was so inspiring, but you held back because
you knew your excitement would draw looks of disapproval? Or
did you ever want to tell your physician (or other person in authority) that his bedside manner stinks and you want to be
treated with the same respect you accord him, but you kept

quiet instead? Last, have you ever wanted to spontaneously dance with your partner at an elegant restaurant because the pianist is playing your song and you are feeling romantic, but you stopped yourself?

> *A limiting belief will cure you of a spontaneous and enthusiastic life.*

These are examples of a cramped and caged spirit that becomes tentative about being authentic and spontaneous. This is what limiting tribal beliefs can do to your life: encourage you to apologize and refrain from expressing your excitement, honesty, and passion.

Are you feeling trapped or constrained in any area of your life? Ask yourself if it's possible that a tribal belief is causing your distress. Are you upset or frustrated by something or someone? Does your life seem too hard or unfair? Are you feeling worn out, like Sisyphus? At the root of your feelings may be an old tribal belief.

Many difficult and uncomfortable feelings are actually caused by tribal beliefs. If you need help seeing what that belief is, ask someone you trust. Often other people can spot our tribal beliefs more easily than we can.

One big clue that you are operating under a tribal belief is if you feel resentment or envy, or feel highly critical of someone. Use your judgments to reveal hidden tribal beliefs. Rachel, for example, let us all know that she has a tribal belief about people contributing to society when she said that a friend of hers "should be doing something better with all that time she has on her hands!" Ron was equally self-revealing when he complained, "Why does he get to take eight weeks vacation a year when I can't find time to get away even for two?"

One easy technique to find out what tribal beliefs you are carrying is to ask yourself some questions that will bring your judgments out in the open:

- What are my judgments toward people who do not share my tribal beliefs about life (or money or marriage or God or . . .)?
- What do I think about people who seem to have it easy in life?
- What do I think about people who seem to have it hard in life?
- What do I think about people who don't seem to take things seriously, or leave one job before they have another?
- What do I think of people who seem to have a lot of happiness in life, or who seem to have everything work out for them?
- How do I feel about people who make mistakes but don't deride themselves?
- What is my opinion of people who don't seem to work hard all the time—or at all?
- And what judgments do I reserve for those people who have a lot of money, have a life of leisure, or who start their own businesses but aren't married to them?

- What about people who divorce? Who divorce more than once? More than twice?
- What do I think about powerful women?
- What do I think about sensitive men?
- What do I think about people who speak up for what they feel, want, or need?
- What about people who aren't willing to sacrifice their health or their happiness for others?

It's important that you know what your judgments are, as these will lead you directly to finding out what tribal beliefs you carry. I'll always remember a man at one of my workshops who told us he wanted to have a lot of money. He said it with an apologetic energy that was instantly evident to me. So I asked him if he had judgments about people with lots of money. "Yes," he replied. "Absolutely. I don't think they're good people. Usually they're selfish." I hope it is abundantly clear that you will not manifest something in your life—like lots of money— if you judge it will make you a bad person or a person of no character!

The irony is that some of what you value the most is based on a limiting belief.

Do you value hard work, service work, happiness, or your spirituality? Listing what you value will help you uncover many tribal beliefs. Following is a list of ideas that many people have strong feelings about. What are yours? Remember that your values come from many sources and can be taught to you without verbal communication. The following phrases may help you see your values more clearly:

My family taught me that money requires _____
My grandparents valued following my dreams unless

_____

My religion teaches me that being a good father
    requires _____

If you are having a hard time answering these questions, try some on-the-spot personal definitions and associations. Don't think of an answer, but listen to the first thing that comes out of your mouth.

- A lazy person is one who _____
- An example of selfishness is _____
- A lousy mother is one who _____
- A true friend is someone who _____
- A flirtatious woman is _____
- Love is for _____
- People who pray are _____

Now jot down your first thoughts as you read the next list. Two very important rules: one, don't judge yourself or your answers, and, two, don't try to be spiritually groovy and give the "correct and socially appropriate" answer. Tell your Truth, even if you deem your answers illogical or don't like them. Until this moment, you probably have been so unaware of many of your criticisms and judgments that you have been clueless that they even *were* judgments.

Remember, many of your beliefs are coming from your unconscious—not your brilliant, logical, caring, unprejudiced, and spiritual self.

Love _____

Friendship _____

Work _____

Money _____

Prosperity _____

Families _____

Grieving _____

Being a good mother _____

Being a good father _____

Marriage _____

Divorce _____

God and spirituality _____

Religion _____

Feeling safe _____

Suffering _____

Worrying _____

Selfishness _____

Asking for help _____

Forgiveness _____

Mistakes _____

Life _____

Happiness _____

Hopes _____

Dreams _____

The nature of women _____

The nature of men _____

Sexuality _____

Childhood _____

Childhood wounding _____

As you uncover your limiting beliefs, you will need to make some choices, especially if you don't like what you uncover. If your limiting belief says *It is selfish to speak up for your needs or ask for what you want,* you are faced with a very limiting choice: to be selfish or not.

Let me give you a small example. A newly married twenty-year-old woman was a guest at her in-laws for dinner. When asked for her favorite part of the turkey, she said, "The dark meat." The truth was, she hated the dark meat and considered it inferior to the white meat. Her limiting belief, however, demanded that she be appropriate and selfless by not asking for what she wanted (the best part of the turkey) but to save it for others.

For the next gazillion years, each time she had any type of fowl, game bird, hen, chicken, turkey, you name it, guess what her father-in-law did for her? He loved her so much and wanted her to be happy and feel so welcome, he always gave her the dark meat.

Once you uncover your limiting belief, see how it plays out

in your daily life. Are you being selfless and compromising on your vacation destination? Are you speaking up in the bedroom? Are your acts of selflessness honoring to you? If not, then can you consider that at times it is necessary—in fact, it makes your friendships easier—to be honest and ask for what you want? Have you ever tried to buy a birthday gift for a friend who has everything or is somewhat fussy? How much easier is it when she tells you what she wants?

Becoming conscious of your beliefs will uncover the conflict inside of you. Becoming aware of the conflict puts you in a position to rewrite your belief and create a new reality with choices that can lead to amazing possibilities in your life. This knowledge will make you powerful, conscious, and able to live your life in alignment with your spirit.

I have compiled the upcoming lists of tribal beliefs from thousands of client readings, many seminars and workshops, TV and radio advertisements, and the clichés and idiomatic expressions used unconsciously in routine conversation. The more I teach, the more I learn about the immense power a tribal belief can have on one's health, happiness, and level of success in life. The deep unconsciousness of these beliefs allows them to stay intact from generation to generation.

If the power of a limiting tribal belief to shape and control your life is nothing short of shocking, the reverse is also true. I have seen people's entire lives start to make sense to them once they uncover their tribal beliefs. Some people feel they need to wait until their parents have passed on to take the plunge and explore their own beliefs. The good news is, it's never too late to reclaim your authenticity, passion, and spontaneity!

It's time now to explore your tribal wallet and do a spring-cleaning. It makes as much sense to weed out the limiting beliefs that make loving and living difficult as it does to get rid of a credit card with high interest.

What's Love Got to Do with It

Tribal beliefs about love can be taught to us in unconventional ways—by history, literature, poetry, TV jingles, even songs. Think about "Stand by Your Man," and "I Can't Live, if Living Is Without You," and "I Will Always Love You," and the multitude of other popular songs that gave us all mixed messages about love. Growing up, a child could get confused by these and wonder whether it's safe to be loved, whether it's safe to pursue love, whether it's worth all the risks. Between the songs, ballads, and literature, we have learned that love is generally painful and can end in despair. To love or not to love, that question causes huge soul conflict and makes great fodder for the psychiatrist's couch.

Judy had dreamed about falling in love from the time she was nine. In fact, she couldn't wait to "stand by her man." On her wedding day, she told me, she cried with happiness. Eight months later, sitting in my office, she was the most unhappy newlywed I had ever met, despite the fact that she truly loved her husband. I found the energetic broadcast of chronic fatigue in her energy field.

Judy had been taught to give and give, and as a result, she was giving more in the marriage than she was receiving, and she worked constantly to find ways to give more. Judy believed *The amount you give is a measure of how deeply you love.*

Yet the more Judy gave, the less she took care of herself, having no energy left to enjoy her life. This pattern leads to chronic fatigue. She could always find something more she should be giving, and she was giving things her spirit didn't really want her to give. For example, when her husband, Larry, wanted to go watch football (a sport Judy didn't enjoy), she went along. When Larry chose a movie, picked a vacation destination, or expressed a sexual preference, Judy acquiesced, even though it was not always what she wanted.

Judy had been raised with the tribal belief that the way to show you love someone is to sacrifice your needs, wants, desires, and even your happiness. Over time, Judy began to disappear as a person. The more she sacrificed her own desires, the more she believed she was showing her love for Larry. But the more she gave, the less she was truly herself. She wasn't listening to her spirit; she was choosing to listen only to her tribal beliefs.

In this short period of time Judy was depleted and had become ill. Her case raises a good point: it doesn't always take a long time to manifest a mind, body, or spiritual illness. It's the **amount** of conflict (feeling torn, resentful, and trapped in your circumstances), the severity of the energy drain (feeling exhausted or worn down by your circumstances), and the choice you make to ignore it all (telling yourself you can handle it, when you know you really can't). Many times after Readings I have heard people say they already knew what I had told them to be true, but they didn't want to know it.

Judy had all but forgotten who she was and what she liked. When Larry asked for a separation, Judy was flabbergasted. She believed she had given all she had (which was true) and the marriage should have worked (according to her tribal beliefs). What had happened was that as Judy became a shell of her former self by denying her soul again and again, Larry started feeling lonely, unchallenged, and bored. He looked around for genuine companionship—and found it elsewhere.

Judy had hit bottom and it was a major wake-up call. It was too late to save her marriage, but not too late to listen to her soul. Although she saw herself as a loving person, the truth is, she was not a loving person toward herself. This fact was made stunningly clear as she realized she gave nothing to herself, but only to others. This particular tribal belief was not the only problem—there was a more deeply hidden one: *To love yourself and take care of your needs is selfish.* This belief caused a tremendous conflict until she rewrote it. In the past, if she took care of herself, her tribal belief said she was a selfish person, when actually feeling resentful and irritable from her lack of self-care was the true selfishness. Now she understood that as a loving person, she could take care of herself and others. This healed her resentment, apathy, and exhaustion. Now that she takes care of herself, her giving energizes her. Her current relationship is much happier.

At fifty-two, Martha was stunning. Although she appeared lively and friendly, she felt empty inside. She had divorced four years earlier. Her loyalty to her tribal belief *True love only comes around once* had condemned her to a life alone. Although friends tried to introduce her to single men, Martha remained aloof. "There's no point in trying," she would exclaim. "I had my turn at love." Martha's belief was so strong, she let it overrule her desire for sex, adventure, friendship, and laughter. She saw these desires merely as wistful longings, not potential realities.

I asked her if loving another person felt good and she nodded. Did it matter if it was true love, or did authentic and intimate and honest love count for anything? She nodded again and I watched the synapses in her brain catapult her to some wonderful conclusions. How fortunate that she chose to examine and rewrite her beliefs!

Although she still believed that true love only comes around once, she recognized that love is always possible. She rewrote her tribal belief to *It is reasonable to believe that although I experienced my one true love in life, I can love another and still be happy—even if I love a little less deeply than the first time.* This minor but significant change in her tribal belief allowed her to begin living again. She was able to take the plunge, joined a singles group, and met a fabulous guy. We now call her Martha the loving jet-setter!

If you have an internal struggle and believe you are not lovable, but crave it deeply, you'll be so conflicted you will feel almost paralyzed. A small modification to a tribal belief like *I am not important, I am not lovable,* or *I am not worth anything* will make all the difference in the world. Consider this possibility—the first step in changing your life: *It is reasonable to believe that I may have been taught things about love by people who didn't know how to love.* This small change can begin your healing process.

I see so many relationships in which people are languishing, losing minute amounts of energy on a daily basis, growing a little more staid, a little more deadened, a little more tired as time goes on. There are many things to consider in ending a relationship, of course, but I always ask people to be honest with themselves about whether the relationship is raising or lowering their vibration. Next, I ask them what role they have played in their relationship (based on tribal beliefs) and how they could change that dynamic.

When you become conscious of why you are staying in the relationship, you don't necessarily have to leave it. You can recover your flagging energy by making the conscious choice to stay and be authentic and take care of yourself. This is an entirely different situation energetically from staying because you are blindly following a tribal belief that says you have no choice. You can stay and be in a healthier place about it. However, if your soul is clearly telling you that you need to leave the relationship, you should listen.

Do you remember the example I gave earlier about the tribal belief *Relationships are hard work* and how having this belief will influence your behavior to create the reality? All tribal beliefs have an element of truth, and therefore seem true. However, as in the game "telephone," the truth has gotten distorted over the years. Is it possible that what you know about relationships is also based on a distorted truth?

"Hey," you say, "relationships *are* a lot of work at times!"

I grant you that, but is it because it's the nature of relationships to be hard? Or is it because tribal beliefs cause people to be inauthentic? How can you be free to speak your truth, or say what you need or want, when these tribal beliefs say otherwise?

- If you can't say something nice, don't say anything at all.
- Taking care of yourself is selfish.
- Be the bigger person and give in during an argument.

I know you've done it: kept what you really think to yourself under the guise of not wanting to hurt the other person. Or not been honest about your needs for fear of being called selfish. Or given in and ignored your deepest desire to keep the peace in a relationship. Under these conditions, which are all based on tribal beliefs, I would agree that a relationship can become work!

What happens when a long-term friendship becomes hard, and you have a tribal belief that says you can't quit a friendship you had since childhood? One of my recent retreats was attended by two women who had been friends since childhood. Sylvia is dynamic, bright, and cheerful. She made friends easily at the retreat and was like a sponge sucking up the information and applying it to her life. Her willingness to look at herself was an inspiration to the group—until it came to her friendship with Marty.

Marty was the polar opposite. Pessimistic and unwilling, she had many excuses for her unhappiness. She was quite unwilling to take responsibility and change any part of her life—what I call poor me, it's not my fault, victim energy. In addition, Marty expected Sylvia to show her loyalty by sharing in her misery. Marty was like a ball and chain around Sylvia's neck. Each time Sylvia began to fly, Marty would drag her back down. Her negativity was suffocating. Whenever Sylvia expressed happiness, Marty became wounded and withdrawn because Sylvia wasn't being a loyal friend. Each evening in their room, Marty would begin a litany of negativity. Without free time to associate with other like-minded individuals (due to her loyalty to Marty), Sylvia began to resent Marty's intrusion on her high-vibration experience in the workshop.

When I mentioned to the group the tribal belief *Long-term friends are friends for life,* I heard a loud energetic sigh from Sylvia. The great *Aha!* had descended upon her. She realized that not only had she outgrown her friendship with Marty, she didn't even *like* her anymore. The moment of awakening occurred at lunch, right after I said my customary prayer of gratitude before the meal.

As I began, Marty loudly pushed her chair back from the table. She was tearful, angry, and quite dramatic. She declared that I had knowingly and maliciously thrown her back into an extremely painful wound from childhood—one that she needed to process before she could continue with the meal. I saw Sylvia roll her eyes and knew that Marty had milked this wounded cow one too many times. Apparently, Marty's father had made them pray before every meal, even in restaurants, which greatly embarrassed her. I gently reminded Marty that it was her option to join the prayer or not. I also pointed out that she was not ten years old anymore and if she felt embarrassed by my prayer, she could leave the table.

Immediately, Marty looked to Sylvia for support. When Sylvia did not respond, Marty left the room in a loud and childish way. Sylvia just shook her head. In that moment, Sylvia made a sacred choice to be true to her spirit. She let go of her tribal belief that *Childhood friends are friends for life.* She accepted that she and Marty were very different people, and they had grown apart a long time ago. She listened to her spirit and ended her draining relationship with Marty, which resulted in a healing and transformative retreat for her.

Kate, a fifty-two-year-old divorcée, yearned for a relationship but claimed there were no available men out there. She stumbled over the belief *Love is only for the young.* She debated, rationalized, appealed to her logic, and finally checked the "No . . . but . . ." box. She looked at me and said, "I don't want that belief," and adamantly denied having it. I chuckled in delight as the great Aha bowled her over.

"Oh my gosh. I do believe that it's harder to find love when you get older."

I nodded, but we couldn't stop there. Next we examined her

tribal beliefs defining "getting older." Her tribe repeatedly drilled it into her that basically life was over at fifty. Well, now, what kind of energetic broadcast do you think Kate was sending out to those available men? "I'm too old for love or fun." Is it any wonder that the men "weren't available"?

Just to lock in Kate's newfound freedom, I reminded her of "Grandma Luge" of the 2006 Winter Olympics. At fifty-two years of age, she was the oldest female athlete to compete in the Olympics! She has friends, a love life, and no one dares to tell her she is too old for anything!

Don't spend a lot of time thinking about the following tribal beliefs list. Trust your initial reaction. Make notes about your conclusions.

When you read each belief, notice what happens inside you, especially down the midline of your body. Does your throat feel tight? Does your stomach clench or hurt? Does your mind counter with "No way, that's ridiculous!" or say "Yes, that's true"? Or, do you hear yourself musing, "No . . . but . . ." If you aren't sure, or you start to play mental Ping-Pong, check off that belief. And if you realize that you are special, and that belief *only holds true for you* but not for the rest of the world, please highlight it with a bright fluorescent marker and consider easing up on yourself.

Your reactions will uncover many of your limiting beliefs.

SOME QUESTIONS TO HELP YOU
UNCOVER YOUR TRIBAL BELIEFS

1. What are your judgments toward people who fall in love easily?
2. What do you think of people who end long-term friendships?
3. Do you think it is harder to find love after a certain age?

TRIBAL BELIEFS ABOUT LOVE AND
FRIENDSHIP

1. Love requires sacrifice.
2. It's important not to trust too easily.
3. True love only comes around once in life—and only if you are lucky.
4. Love is painful.
5. Love isn't for everyone.
6. Love is only for the young.
7. Love wanes over time.
8. The amount you give is a measure of how deeply you love.
9. If those you love reject you, you are nothing.
10. Good relationships require a lot of work.
11. A long-term friend should stay your friend for life.
12. Never deny a request for help from a friend.
13. Relationships are hard.
14. Never break a promise to a friend, no matter what.

15. Don't tell a friend the truth if it will hurt their feelings.
16. Commitment means suffocation.
17. If your own mother gives you up for adoption, then you must not be lovable.

Going to the Chapel

I couldn't talk about love without including marriage, a relationship based on a sacred vow. Such a vow is not to be taken lightly, but many people have the tribal belief that marriage is forever *no matter what.* Can you imagine the effects of this belief on a woman married to an abusive man? Battered and abused, should she continue to allow a tribal belief to trap her? Sadly, many people—including women in this situation—would answer, "Yes."

Cathy thought she had married the love of her life—until their fifth anniversary. Bill was nice, polite, and an all-around good husband and provider. Everyone seemed to like him. Unfortunately, he was also emotionally unavailable and Cathy was very lonely. They tried counseling and Catholic marriage encounters, but Bill preferred to think rather than feel.

After the birth of their first child, Cathy thought she could ignore the loneliness and focused on her son. It was a lovely distraction during the day. Unfortunately, the nights were too long. It was so lonely for Cathy to lie in bed with someone who felt no connection with her, she began taking painkillers to escape the hurt. Due to the tribal belief *Divorcées are failures,* she felt trapped in her loveless marriage. Sometimes their politeness with each other was so painful she wanted to scream. How could she explain divorcing a nice person? She had all the material comforts she needed. She was secure and protected by Bill. He was so good to her, how could she leave him? She'd have to be crazy, she thought. But she dreamed of divorce daily and felt guilty about it.

Cathy's guilt plagued her. When her son began school the loneliness returned with a vengeance. Soon after, she was addicted to painkillers. She struggled with the knowledge that her husband was a great guy—so why was she so unhappy and lonely all the time? As the relationship continued, her spirit was muted and she occasionally thought that dying would be much easier than living.

We discussed her tribal belief that leaving her marriage did not make her a failure, but she was adamant and refused to consider any other possibilities. Bill steadfastly refused to acquire any emotional depth. His job was to provide for his family, and he was good at his job. He could not see what the problem was.

Cathy's guilt finally got the better of her. She still couldn't understand how her marriage could fail when she was married to such a nice person. She convinced herself that she was too needy, and she gradually shut down her emotions and her needs. Anger and resentment simmered inside of her each time she saw a happy and loving couple.

A diagnosis of intestinal cancer marked her twelfth anniversary. She was not even upset about it. In fact, she seemed relieved. She found it easier to die from her insides rotting than to change her tribal belief. But how can you commend loyalty that results in a needless death?

Another reason people stay in unhealthy marriages is concern for their reputations. The problem is rampant and stems partly from the lack of authenticity I spoke of earlier in this chapter when we were talking about love. Is life so unprecious a gift that you would sacrifice or trade it for a good reputation? Is it a matter of life and death for you to be considered a good wife, daughter, husband, son, or human being?

I wish I could only tell you about clients who have been able to change their beliefs and thrive, but that would not be honest. I want to tell you the truth about the power of tribal beliefs: they can make your life a daily joy or a daily grind.

Randi was married for twelve years to a man who was a recovering alcoholic. Unfortunately, his recovery didn't change his blueprint. His negative patterns of communication, his unspoken resentments, and his bouts of deep depression had marred their marriage. But Randi hung in there, saying she was learning detachment and spiritual maturity, as she coped with chronic fatigue. Although she had entertained the idea of a divorce, her strong tribal beliefs—*Marriage is forever, no matter what,* and *People who divorce are failures; they didn't try hard enough*—kept her in the marriage.

Randi came to my workshop and I saw her profound conflict. As I was teaching a group about the power of a limiting belief, I suddenly turned to her and asked: "Do you plan to continue giving up your energy, happiness, and health for a tribal belief about marriage that you don't even agree with?"

Randi almost fell out of her chair. She immediately recognized the conflict between her loyalty to her family's beliefs and her soul that wanted to love again. She began to rewrite her limiting belief and broke down in tears in gratitude. She asked me to Read her—to see if her new belief, *It's reasonable to believe that even good people end up in marriages that should end,* ran through her energy system. I said, "Randi, it not only runs through your energy system, but also the system of all the people sitting at your table." Her epiphany was so powerful it literally changed her blueprint in the moment. She was coming to a place of absolute truth, and I saw that some of her tablemates were shocked and shaken, but some had gotten the kick in the pants they needed to kick-start their life. At the break, many people thanked Randi for her courage, and she shyly admitted that she never thought of herself as courageous.

But courage was a prominent part of her energetic blueprint. She did have the ability to take risks and inspire others. As if her transformation wasn't enough, moments later she jumped out of her chair exclaiming, "I never really liked him anyway; I got married because my parents really liked him. Within a year, I knew I had made a terrible mistake but thought I had no options. I've been feeling guilty all these years. Now I understand—I was trying to force myself to become someone I'm not. The truth is, I want a divorce."

Her moment of truth had burst open the door of healing. All of the self-recrimination began to dissolve as she reclaimed her power and spoke what was true in her heart. Her moment of complete integrity allowed her to accept the role she had played in her unhappiness. Understanding her role—becoming spiritually responsible—was the first step toward self-forgiveness and had a profound ripple effect on others in the workshop.

Acknowledging the voice of your spirit without apology or self-judgment can burst open the door to your healing.

A moment of pure truth can be felt around a room. When someone's words completely match their energy, they emanate true power, and it is this power that ignited the room. Randi had listened to her spirit without judgment or apology, and thus the room responded in kind. Her vibrant energy was uncontainable, and when she met up with friends weeks later, they were astounded at the change in her. One of them even said, "I thought you had chronic fatigue?" Randi replied, "Not anymore!"

Moments like these will change your life in an instant; it is a form of spontaneous healing and is beautiful to witness. Acknowledging the voice of your spirit without apology or judgment will do the same for you!

SOME QUESTIONS TO HELP YOU UNCOVER YOUR TRIBAL BELIEFS

1. Are you critical of someone who has been married more than twice?
2. Is it better not to marry at all rather than divorce?
3. Is it ever okay to end a marriage?

TRIBAL BELIEFS ABOUT MARRIAGE AND DIVORCE

1. Marriage is forever.
2. You can't end a marriage until you have tried everything.

3. If your marriage fails, it's because you failed your husband/wife.
4. You shouldn't divorce a nice guy/gal.
5. You can't leave someone when they are sick.
6. If you hurt someone by ending a relationship, you should feel badly for as long as they are hurting.
7. Divorced people are promise breakers and failures.
8. If your marriage fails, it's because you didn't try hard enough.
9. Children are better off with two parents, even if they are terribly unhappy in their marriage.
10. A good person can make a marriage work.

Work Comes First

Can you guess how many people have told me that logically they do not believe they must work hard to make good money, yet they remain loyal to the tribal belief *Financial success comes only from hard work?* Too, too many. I watch people like this work themselves to exhaustion seven days a week, and I ask them, "How does that explain the people who become successful *without* keeping their nose to the grindstone?"

Most managers in the corporate world come in early and leave late. They work fifty, even sixty hours a week in an attempt to get ahead in the company. But I know a woman who was a manager at a Fortune 500 high-tech company who rewrote her beliefs about working hard to *It's reasonable to believe that I can be successful without giving up the rest of my life.* She embraced her new belief a little bit at a time. She began by changing her hours. Karen came in at 9:00 and left at 5:00 or 5:30 every day. Next, she made sure to always take a lunch break and committed to not taking work home with her, and she said no to projects that would have overloaded her. Her newfound energy and excitement at work allowed her creativity and productivity to flourish.

When it came time for her performance review, some of her peers looked forward to seeing her get her comeuppance. But Karen received the very highest rating the company awarded. Why? Because she did a great job! Her department produced top-notch results, she had zero staff turnover, and she was liked and respected by the teams she worked with. It didn't matter to top management how she pulled this off; it just mattered that she did. What was Karen's secret? She focused on managing her time well, put effort only into issues that really mattered, listened to her people, skipped the office politicking, and spoke up passionately when something important was being overlooked. In other words, because she knew she had only forty hours to get everything done—and done well—she worked smart, not hard.

Ask yourself this: What kind of success do you think you deserve, and how hard do you think you have to work for it? Remember, we are meant to be in the flow, to live according to our energetic blueprint, and to embrace all the good that comes to us when we stop being who we are *not* and start shining as we are. Even if you are able to work hard, does it genuinely feel good to do so? Must you earn your success by working really hard, or is it okay for success to come easily? It's essential that you acknowledge your beliefs about success if your reality is going to change.

There's another tribal belief about work that you may have heard: *If you are not working hard, you are not a good member of society.* In other words, you are a lazy and unproductive human being. Now imagine you have lived a good life. You have coached your son's baseball team, been a fair boss, and contributed to the world's betterment. Then you lose your job or reach the age of mandatory retirement. Your pain is caused much more by your limiting tribal belief than the loss of your job. All of a sudden, a lifetime of self-esteem (which was based on your performance at work) goes down the drain. Now you regard yourself as an unproductive and worthless human being, and that hurts.

Jerry faced a similar dilemma. His boss loved him because he was a hard worker who for fourteen years rarely missed a day, took few vacations, and was always available for overtime. Then Jerry hurt his back and was unable to work. He now became—in his own eyes—a lazy and nonproductive human being. He tried desperately to continue working, to the detriment of the herniated disc in his back. Then he tried to ignore the pain, and eventually he ended up taking excessive amounts of Vicodin just to function. I imagine you know where this is going. His tribal belief was so powerful, it was less stressful for him to be addicted than to miss work and believe himself a worthless person.

Eventually, his pain was so great he was forced to go on disability. Fortunately for Jerry, his wife didn't see him as less than a man. Her support helped him return to school and train as a counselor helping drug-addicted teens, something he had a natural aptitude for. As his rigid adherence to his old belief healed, so did his pain.

The work ethic taught you by your tribe members may have been shaped by their unique troubles, disasters, misfortune, and fears. Whatever their painful situation, times have changed. Do you want to accept this legacy and pass it on—unexamined— to your children? Or do you want to consult your soul and create your own beliefs about work, its role in your life, and how much effort you need to make to succeed?

I'll never forget one of my students, Lily, who told me, "My gosh, I've been working according to the beliefs of my ancestors who were Irish potato farmers. They really did have to carry boulders out of the fields—I feel like I've been doing the same thing." While she wasn't literally carrying rocks, I saw heavy energetic ones she carried daily, because of her limiting belief *If you don't work hard, you can't survive.* Lily still carries a few rocks in her knapsack, but they are quickly turning into pebbles.

I know a therapist who was appalled when she discovered she had a princess archetype (an inherent part of her blueprint that liked to be pampered, treated as special by men, and looked good in pink, even though she prided herself on her independence). She was a strong, assertive, bright, and accomplished professional who simply could not accept that she was also a delicate princess—she could take care of herself. She had many tribal beliefs about the importance and value of hard work, sacrifice, and earning her own way. As as result, she worked hard in her practice and attracted many clients who were resistant, difficult, and hard to work with. She felt very successful being a hard worker and was doing a great job of upholding her tribals. Princess energy (allowing herself to kick back and be pampered) just did not fit with her concept of a good person.

But she was open-minded and started to admit that, yes, she did like being taken care of on occasion and that, secretly, the idea of not working so hard all the time really did have some appeal. It took some work on her part because her tribals were so entrenched, but she started to dress more femininely and then began to fire those difficult clients. At the same time, she was changing her tribal beliefs and accepting that she could have value as a person outside of working all the time. It took about nine months, but her practice transformed; she cut her workweek down so she had more time to relax and regenerate. Without her difficult clients, she had much more energy to enjoy her life. She learned a different meaning of success. Thanks to more free time, she followed her intuition and went on a trip to South America (against all her old tribals of never taking a real vacation) and met a wonderful man who lived less than an hour away from her. He really loves taking care of her, and she really enjoys him doing so—so much so, they are getting married this summer.

Consider one more important thing regarding tribal beliefs about work. Some people are meant to have many careers in a lifetime, or wander from experience to experience, never settling down or taking the traditional route of college, career, marriage, children, retirement. Some souls are meant to explore, to be free spirits, or to give up everything in midlife to do something entirely different. If you are one of these folks and you are not following your spirit, you need to rewrite your tribal beliefs about work and life; otherwise you will feel trapped and resigned—two emotions that begin the decline into illness.

SOME QUESTIONS TO HELP YOU UNCOVER YOUR TRIBAL BELIEFS

1. Would you ever consider taking a sabbatical?
2. What do you think of people who take mental health days off when they aren't sick?
3. Does work require effort?
4. Do you feel more valuable when you are working hard?
5. How do you know when you have worked hard enough?
6. What would you consider an acceptable excuse to cut back on your work schedule: feeling stressed; serious illness; death?

TRIBAL BELIEFS ABOUT WORK

1. If you don't work hard, you will never succeed.
2. Things are worth more if you've worked hard to get them.
3. Work comes before fun.
4. If you haven't worked hard for something, it has little value.
5. If you don't work hard, you are a lazy or unproductive member of society.
6. It takes five years to succeed in business.

7. Once you've found a secure job you should stay in it.

8. Never quit a job until you have another one lined up.

9. Sabbaticals are simply excuses to goof off.

10. Working hard makes you a good person.

11. You have to work long hours to succeed.

12. Working hard for everything you get is something to be proud of.

13. You aren't worthy of anything unless you're working like a dog.

14. Idle hands are the devil's workshop.

Prosperity Is Only for the Rich

Since prosperity begins in your energy system, the first step in attaining prosperity is to change your limiting tribal beliefs about money. It's not about how much money you have, but how neutral you feel about having it, spending it, how much it's okay to have, and what you should do with it to be considered a good person. Prosperity requires you to have a good relationship with money: First, you cannot assign power or status to it—this requires true self-esteem. And second, you cannot apologize for wanting it, having it, or spending it. How can you easily manifest money if it makes you uncomfortable, you have judgment on making too much too easily, or you have to work yourself to death to get it?

Wouldn't it be better to rewrite your limiting beliefs about money rather than let them determine the amount of money you will have in your lifetime?

We often hear people say, "Money doesn't grow on trees." Underlying that old saying are the tribal beliefs *Money is scarce* and *Money is hard to get*. I have worked with multimillionaires who never felt they had enough money. They could never enjoy their wealth, beautiful homes, cars, or luxury travel. Like Ebenezer Scrooge, they were misers of enjoyment and life. Acutely aware of getting their money's worth, they easily feel ripped off.

The amount of energy they spend on tightly hording their money leaves them angry, distrustful, and unable to enjoy the freedom that money buys. I've also noticed that these are the people who chronically undertip and feel resentful at having to leave anything at all. I actually observed one man insistent on using his Triple A discount for an ice cream cone at Dairy Queen.

When you buy into scarcity beliefs, you set yourself up to undergo hardship in order to obtain money—perhaps by working long hours or "paying your dues" in some other way. If you think money is scarce, you have to hold on to it very tightly and be very cautious with it. Eventually money becomes a thing of power and, yes, an energetic drain because it's always on your mind.

If your energy broadcasts that there is never enough money to go around, I promise you that this will become your reality.

Just when you have some money in the bank, your transmission will fail. Just when you get ahead on your bills, a crisis will occur. The ripple effect of this belief is that when you fear the lack of money, you will hold on quite tightly and not share it or contribute it to worthy and needy causes. This will color and impact all arenas of your life, as well as the lives of others who could have been helped. And if you apologize for having money, you will invite judgment from others. Scarcity and apology energy are rooted in tribal beliefs about money and safety.

I worked with a marvelous gentleman who was diagnosed with prostate cancer. When I did a Reading on Vince, I saw that he had made some poor financial investments and put his money in firms that went bankrupt. However, the actual financial loss was not what helped instigate his prostate cancer. Rather, it was Vince's belief that *A man needs money to be powerful.* Thus, when he lost his money, he lost his power. Vince became impotent—or so he believed—in the world of men. This affected all his relationships, including his relationship with himself. He lost his self-esteem and, eventually, his courage. Vince could no longer use his money to buy friendships, approval, sex, love, or attention. With this kind of energy drain, it would have been very difficult for him to heal from the cancer. He needed to find his inherent worth.

Vince worked diligently on rewriting his beliefs about money and discovered that his real power was in his sense of humor, sensitivity, and creativity. Freed from feeling powerless, he used his creativity to create a new financial empire and is having fun doing it. Because his desire for money now comes from a clean motivation—he simply enjoys the creative process to attain it—he is even more successful and, at present, free of cancer.

Some tribes have the belief *It's not okay for me to enjoy my money when people I love don't have as much.* I know a man, a hardworking and gifted hairdresser, who gave most of his money to his family. David rarely spent anything on himself, had little saved for retirement, and felt guilty having money when his family didn't. He was physically exhausted, neglected himself, and wasn't able to take time off from work to recover. His belief was clearly a burden as he remarked, "It didn't seem fair that I made money so easily; it just felt wrong to keep it." The real problem, however, was that David could never give enough to his family to appease his guilt. Only changing his limiting belief would do that.

Marcia is as uncomfortable with money as David. She is quite wealthy through marriage and apologized for her wealth continually. She felt she did not deserve to live so easily and donated to charitable organizations to even the score. Unfortunately, her donations were tainted by her unclean motivation to ease her guilt for being wealthy. This guilt sent out a broadcast of apology energy that invited judgment and criticism from others who implied she should be donating more.

For a while, she immersed herself in the social charity scene, hoping to buy redemption for marrying into money. Her redemption never came, and she told me that sometimes she thought that giving up her money would solve her feelings of guilt. I told her that giving up her money would not solve her problem. Changing her tribal beliefs around wealth would eliminate her apology energy and resolve her guilt, allowing her to enjoy her money.

Marcia immediately recognized some tribal beliefs she had:

- Rich people are selfish—that is probably how they became rich.
- Money earned through hard work is admirable; inherited or married money is not.
- Having money requires you to give generously.
- It's not okay to enjoy your money—that's selfish.
- It's not okay to have so much when so many have so little.

Marcia felt the energy drain each time she spoke these tribals aloud. I asked her to listen to her spirit about her money. She was suddenly overcome with tears and managed to whisper how grateful she was for her good fortune. Her spirit spoke again, saying it was okay to have such a nice life—she didn't have to earn it, pay for it; she simply deserved it. The last urgings of her spirit were more like a gentle kick in the pants saying, "Knock it off and enjoy what you have."

Marcia wasted no time rewriting her beliefs in accordance with her spirit and sheepishly acknowledged she was embarrassed by her behavior. I told her she could waste more time beating herself up, or she could be courageous and heal her spirit. With each rewrite, she became more at ease with her money and had less conflict with her soul. Now when she donates money, her motivation is clean—she isn't giving from a place of guilt, but rather a desire to help others. She gives what she is comfortable with and moves on. Now she understands my message that money buys freedom, and she enjoys the money she has.

SOME QUESTIONS TO HELP YOU UNCOVER YOUR TRIBAL BELIEFS

1. Do you believe it is unfair that some people make so much money?
2. If you tithe, why do you do it?
3. If you were left an inheritance, what would you do with it?
4. Do you resent people who have more than you do?

TRIBAL BELIEFS ABOUT MONEY

1. Money doesn't grow on trees.
2. There's never enough money to go around.
3. Save for a rainy day—but when it rains, try not to use your savings.
4. Loss of money equals loss of power.
5. You have to work hard to earn money.
6. If you have money, you have to even the score by giving to others who have less.
7. If you have money, don't flaunt it.
8. Rich people are selfish—that's probably how they became rich.
9. Money earned through hard work is admirable. Inherited money is not.

10. If you have money, you have a duty to give generously.
11. It's not okay to enjoy your money—that's selfish.
12. Money is what makes a man (or a woman) powerful.
13. Money is hard to come by.
14. Money shouldn't come easily.

I want to say one more thing about money and prosperity before we move on, and it has to do with positive affirmations. I could fill another book or two with all the positive affirmations people have told me they recite daily. Do you know that a single tribal belief can cancel out every one of your affirmations before it has even left your mouth? The following story focuses on the area of prosperity, but the principles apply to any area of your life where you want to succeed.

A wonderful young man told me in a workshop that one of his affirmations was "I am a money magnet." I took one look at his energetic blueprint and said, "Honey, you're no money magnet, but you're quite a babe magnet!" He was shocked, to say the least.

Riley is good-looking, has a loving and genuine spirit, and is the kind of person you just feel better being around. Engaged to a wonderful woman, he was aghast at what I told him. His upbringing taught him *Once you're engaged, it's wrong to exude sensuality or attract anyone but your intended.* So Riley was busy suppressing his natural babe-magnet energy and focusing on making money. He wanted to be a good provider for his fiancée, and he believed his prosperity affirmations would help him.

Unfortunately, Riley's affirmations were violating the first principle of prosperity: embrace who you are and stop trying to be someone else. Riley is an absolute doll. That's who he is. But he was trying to suppress it, thinking it was wrong to be attractive to others now that he was engaged. It took a huge amount of his energy to deny who he really was: a major babe magnet, not a money magnet!

What do I mean by saying Riley was a babe magnet? Simply that people were attracted to him, they liked being around him, they liked his energy. People find him safe, sensitive, and strong. He doesn't use his energy to manipulate or control others, and he is a person of very high integrity. I saw that these qualities had brought him clients and would bring him even more in the future—and thus more income—once he embraced them. Riley's energetic blueprint would create prosperity for him; he didn't have to work so hard at it. I told him to cut out the prosperity affirmations and to accept that he was a babe magnet.

This was hard for Riley, but it delighted his fiancée, who loved him dearly and genuinely wanted him to shine. As Riley started to accept his attractiveness, his self-esteem grew. (It always does once you stop trying to be who you are not and embrace who you are.) Of course, as his confidence grew, so did his business.

Putting enormous amounts of energy into fighting your soul's wisdom is a direct cause of the lack of prosperity, happiness, or the full success you seek. You cannot achieve prosperity by fighting who you really are. As soon as you embrace your true self, however, all your energy begins to flow freely in a direction that increases your self-esteem and brings you the opportunities you need.

Blood Is Thicker Than Water

What can I say about families? I've heard this many times from clients: "I can't stand my family, but I have to see them on the holidays." When I ask if they would visit a boss or neighbor they couldn't stand, they reply, "And ruin my holiday? No way!"

Family represents the tribe. Breaking a tribal law is tantamount to heresy—you are bucking the tribe and being disloyal. To the tribe it feels like a betrayal, yet if you were to attach yourself to a vibration meter and measure your vibration when in the company of that family you can't stand, what do you think it would show? I can assure you it doesn't show much.

I've often wanted to take a video camera into a workshop and preserve some of the unbelievable moments when people defend their tribal beliefs. One time I asked a gentleman why he was spending Thanksgiving with family members he couldn't stand (a visit that always left him sick for three days afterward). He answered, "Because holidays are for family time, not having fun." At another workshop, I met Susan, who didn't say much but spoke volumes energetically. I saw she was being abused, both emotionally and physically, by her husband. Her silence was the product of a tribal belief that said *Don't air your dirty laundry in public, it will shame the family.* That belief had kept her a prisoner of abuse for nearly four years. That workshop was the beginning of her freedom.

Imagine you are taught to love your parents, siblings, spouse, or children no matter what, and all because *they are family.* The way to show your love is clearly defined: spend time with them, talk with them on the phone when you can't be with them, do kind things for them, and support them during a crisis. Imagine that your family raises your vibration. One that benefits your spirit, your happiness, even your health. You enjoy Sunday dinners with them and make it a tradition; you celebrate one another's accomplishments and lend a helping hand when needed. Loving your family always includes lots of laughter and intimacy, and being with them raises your vibration. This is an example of when a tribal belief is good for your spirit.

Now, however, imagine the same tribal belief but a different family. One that maybe drinks too much or is quick to criticize, where comments quickly turn to hurtful arguments and judgments, and your successes and efforts to be a better person ignite disdain because you aren't like the rest of the family.

What if your soul is saying, "Please don't go to these family gatherings," but your tribal belief says you must attend to show you care? How are you going to choose?

Julie's father has been distant and emotionally dead for all of her life. He is incapable of intimacy. He talks endlessly about his hobby: clock repair. All conversations with him involve detailed information about bezels and other incredibly boring and tedious information, of interest to no one except those genuinely interested in clock repair. The truth is, Julie's father has no capacity for bonding, intimacy, or meaningful conversation.

Although he was exposed for twenty-five years to asbestos, and smoked for many of those same years, he continues to work in a moldy damp basement workshop and does not use an air filter, exercise, or eat particularly healthily. The only clock-free conversations Julie has been able to have with him involve her haranguing him to take better care of himself.

As the oldest daughter and a nurse, she had many tribals telling her this was her role. Over the Christmas holiday, she spent only a little time with him, refusing his invitations to visit and spend time together. At long last, she did not feel guilty taking herself out of a situation that had always left her feeling dead and heavy.

Two weeks later, he was hospitalized with pneumonia. When Julie got the news, she immediately felt guilty for not spending more time with her dad. She sent him an air purifier but was wrestling with her feelings of agitation, wondering if she should fly across the country to be with him, take a leave of absence from her job, or be otherwise helpful to her dad.

Upon honest exploration, however, Julie admitted that she felt little worry about her father. In fact, she felt nothing for him except sadness for his self-imposed plight. She had no real connection with him. What was tearing her up inside was her tribal belief *A good daughter should drop everything in her life to take care of an ailing parent.* This is a perfect example of a tribal belief in terrible conflict with one's soul. At a soul level, Julie knew she had no real relationship with her father. She knew that being around him brought her down terribly and lowered her vibration. She also knew there was nothing she could do to be helpful to someone intent on slow self-destruction.

When Julie named the tribal belief that was causing her agitation, she visibly relaxed. When she let herself speak the truth about her lack of desire to intervene in her father's situation, her agitation disappeared altogether. As she rewrote her tribal belief, she began to know at a gut level that she was indeed a good daughter even though she did not participate in the tribal belief requirement of being upset for her father. Her new tribal belief was *A good daughter takes care of herself even if her parents make poor choices.*

While the situation with Julie's father was indeed sad, it no longer had a hold on her or made her unhappy. She has pulled back her power from a tribal belief that was hurting her, and she's started to focus her energies on her own life, including her growing career. She now honors him by letting him live his life the way he chooses. She speaks briefly on the phone with him on occasion and acknowledges to herself that she is still a good daughter even though she won't sacrifice her life for her father.

People often excuse the horrible behavior of a parent by saying, "But he's my father" or "But she's my mother." It's as if they believe that parents have the right to undermine and injure their children, and children have a duty to put up with it. They don't!

It's not uncommon for clients to want to talk to their therapist at length about how they have "learned to process their reactions" to being around an abusive parent, or how they can now "be with themselves" while in creepy family situations. What is clear, however, is that these clients are trying to hang on to the tribal belief *Honor thy mother and father no matter what* by talking themselves into thinking they are okay spending time with someone who hurts them. Sadly, the energy drain caused by trying to be with someone you don't like being around, someone who lowers your vibration, is huge. It can prove very costly to your health. Talking won't heal it; changing your tribal belief will.

The tribal belief *Honor thy mother and father* (with its often-unspoken subtext, *no matter what*) has caused people to suffer terribly. I have comforted the daughters and sons of narcissistic parents, abusive parents, distant or emotionally absent parents, and just plain cruel parents. Such parents can continue to terrorize a child well into adulthood. Afraid to dishonor the parent or disgrace the family, the person quietly bears the damage done. Rigidly adhering to this tribal belief has led to the loss of love, happiness, and passion in a person's adult life. Consider these people:

- The man who stays in a job he hates to please a parent.
- The woman who gets married to please her parents even though she thrives on being single.
- The couple who produce grandchildren even though they have no desire for kids.
- Adult sons or daughters who are gay but have to hide their lifestyle and their soul mate for fear of their parents' rejection.

We have all heard about children whose parents have been convicted of a terrible crime saying, "Of course I still love him, he's my father." If they really meant it, I could accept their statement. But I see that their energy is flat and gray. I know they are forcing themselves to adhere to a tribal belief that says *You have to love your parents no matter what* or *Family are people you love even if you don't like them.*

SOME QUESTIONS TO HELP YOU UNCOVER YOUR TRIBAL BELIEFS

1. Do you have judgments about siblings who don't speak to each other?
2. Do you value peace in your family above all else?
3. Do you think it's wrong for a family member to financially succeed and not share with the rest of the family?

TRIBAL BELIEFS ABOUT FAMILIES

1. Blood is thicker than water (so stand by your family no matter what they do or say).
2. If your own mother doesn't love you, no one will.
3. Holidays should be spent with your family.
4. Give in to keep the peace in the family.
5. Good daughters/sons take care of their parents no matter what.
6. Nonblood relatives or friends will never be as dependable as your "real" family.
7. It's selfish to be happy when your family isn't.
8. Keep the family secrets at all costs.

9. When the chips are down, your family is the only place you can turn to or trust.

10. Taking care of yourself before your family is selfish.

11. Families stick together and take care of each other, no matter what.

12. You can't have an easy life if your family doesn't.

13. What's cooked at home is eaten at home.

14. Honor your mother and father no matter what.

15. You owe it to your parents to take care of them in their old age.

16. A good son or daughter should drop everything in his or her life to take care of an ailing parent.

17. Family loyalty is more important than taking care of yourself.

18. If your mother gave you up for adoption, you are not lovable, and no one else will ever love you.

Mom and Dad

In Chapter 1, I told you about Debra, who believed *A good wife should never be more successful than her husband.* How many women refuse to shine brightly because they aren't supposed to outshine their husbands? Too, too many. Trapped by a toxic tribal belief, they believe it is their job to promote their husbands, not themselves. When I consider the legacy they are leaving their children, I shudder. What if one of their daughters has the genius and desire to be an innovative researcher working on a cure for cancer, but she's married to an unsuccessful lawyer or a man who's content raising the children?

This is only one of the many tribal beliefs about being a good wife. However, there are an even greater number of tribal beliefs about what good mothers are supposed to think, feel, and do!

Dottie believed *Love means doing everything for your children.* Whenever her adult children were in trouble, she gave them money. When they were thrown out of their apartment, she let them live with her. Dottie did this despite the fact that her kids were ungrateful, abusive, and not bonded to their mom. When I asked her why she allowed them to treat her like that, she replied: "They are my children, and a loving mother is supposed to do everything for them." This tribal belief gives Dottie the privilege of being abused, yelled at, taunted, threatened, and kicked around. When she broke her hip and was unable to walk, her daughter, Susan, sat downstairs and watched television, unwilling to cook. When Dottie hired a housekeeper to cook and clean for her during her convalescence, Susan complained about the cost of the housekeeper and lamented there would be no inheritance left for her.

What's ironic is that Dottie was a fireball in a man's world. She worked her way up the corporate ladder, tolerating no disrespect from anyone in her department. She was successful in business and financially secure, but in her family life she was a prisoner of her own device. When I asked Dottie why she allowed Susan to treat her so brutally, her response was, "She's my daughter. What else can I do?"

The weight of Dottie's tribal beliefs came crashing down

upon her the following summer when she developed lung cancer and was put on oxygen at home. Dottie's friends tried to convince her to kick her daughter out and change the locks because of her daughter's cruel behavior, but Dottie wouldn't do it. When friends found her, she was lying in bed emaciated—she hadn't eaten in three days—and gasping for breath. Her oxygen had been turned off. Susan claimed she had turned the oxygen off to move it and forgot to turn it back on again. For three days she hadn't noticed her mother's shortness of breath. When asked why her mother was starving, Susan said she had simply been too busy to cook for her mom.

I know many of you will read this story and think it can't be true. Sadly, it is. You probably wonder why Dottie didn't change the locks and be done with her daughter. For those of you without the belief *A mother does everything for her children*, Dottie's behavior sounds outrageous, but to her, there was no choice. Even though she was aware of her tribal belief, she refused to rewrite it or consider that it was harmful to her. She died shortly thereafter.

Are your tribal beliefs worth dying for?

SOME QUESTIONS TO HELP YOU UNCOVER YOUR TRIBAL BELIEFS

1. What kind of mother raises an unhappy child?
2. Can you be happy if your child is not?
3. Is it your fault if your child ends up on drugs?
4. Does caring for your children demand sacrifice from a mother?

TRIBAL BELIEFS ABOUT BEING A GOOD
MOTHER

1. My children's needs always come first.
2. A good woman takes care of her husband and family before herself.
3. A good mother is responsible for her children's happiness.
4. A good mother does everything for her children.
5. If children are not happy or successful, the mother has failed.
6. A good mother can motivate her children to change.
7. You are only as happy in life as your least happy child (said by Charlie Gibson on *Good Morning America*, quoting his wife).
8. A good mother is always patient.
9. A good mother stays home with her children.

Jon is the sweetest guy you'll ever meet. He's kind, thoughtful, loving, and good—to everyone but himself. He struggles with feelings of inadequacy as a father, a husband, and a man. He believes he is responsible for his family's happiness and welfare. Should they have problems, it's his job to sort it out, fix it, or criticize himself for his failure.

Jon yearns for more passion and fun in his life. At a workshop I watched him blossom into a relaxed and happy guy—he had the weekend off from taking care of everyone else's needs. Jon is unhappy and depressed. He feels trapped and unable to live his own life, yet he also feels guilty that he wants to shirk his family duties. When I did a Reading on him, I saw a man young at heart who was aging quickly. He was also on the road to developing diabetes; he was already feeling tired most of the time.

I Read several tribal beliefs in Jon's energetic blueprint that were causing a conflict with his soul and draining his energy:

- A good man takes care of his family, no matter what.
- A good man takes care of his family and friends before himself.
- A good husband provides for all the needs and wants of his wife.
- It's a father's job to provide for all his children's needs.

It was obvious to me that Jon was (consciously or unconsciously) trying to control his reputation. He wanted power over how other people thought of him. People with this issue will compromise themselves, ignore their own needs, keep silent, and put up with a lot just to save face. I have watched such people churn silently, resentment eating them alive, just to keep their reputation intact. This is exactly what Jon did.

Jon's reputation within the community was of utmost concern to him. His need to be known as a good man was stronger than any intuition or guidance coming from his soul or from God.

Another client, Mark, had a deceptively simple tribal belief: *A good father provides everything for his children or else he is a bad father.*

Mark worked overtime consistently and did without to pay for his children's cars, college tuition, and new clothes. He bought them things on credit, things he could not afford. He had gotten himself in a world of debt and longed for the freedom to take a vacation or do something for himself, but his children always came first. Naturally, his energetic broadcast had taught his children that all they had to do was say, "Oh, I wish I had a new stereo," and Dad would buy it for them.

Mark's other predominant belief was *Children should never want for anything.* To Mark's way of thinking, when kids wanted for things, it implied that their father was a poor provider, thus a poor father and a bad person. Like Jon, Mark could not bear to have a reputation as a bad father, especially not in his children's eyes. He was held hostage by his fear that if he said no to any of their wants or needs, his kids would think badly of him.

So Mark worked longer and longer hours and ignored his needs for rest. His tribal belief about being a good and honorable father drove him to pick up extra jobs in addition to the sixty hours he already worked.

Once he looked at how his limiting beliefs had driven him to exhaustion, he started to rewrite them. It was tough because he really wanted to be a good dad. I suggested he consider, *A good dad provides love and limits for his children.* It got Mark thinking out of the box and led to other beliefs that changed the nature of his relationship with his children, bringing them much closer.

SOME QUESTIONS TO HELP YOU
UNCOVER YOUR TRIBAL BELIEFS

1. What do you think about a father who says no to his children?
2. Should a good father give his children everything he didn't get as a child?
3. Can you be a good father and not spend a lot of time with your children?

TRIBAL BELIEFS ABOUT BEING A GOOD
FATHER

1. A good man works his hardest for his family and provides everything they need.
2. A good man thinks of himself last.
3. Being productive is the sign of a good man.
4. A good father will do anything to make his children happy.
5. If your children are not happy or successful, you have failed.
6. A good father provides everything for his children.
7. A good father can't be happy unless his children are happy.
8. A good father doesn't complain or get angry, and he works hard.

Healing 101

Tribal beliefs are so powerful they can change the course of your illness. Janet was afflicted with an incurable disease. When I asked her if she would consider a spontaneous healing, do you know what she said? "No." Do you want to know why? Because she had the tribal belief *I have to earn everything I get,* and she didn't feel like she had earned her healing at that time. Later, after changing her tribal belief and recognizing that, yes, she deserved grace, she experienced a complete healing.

Then there are the tribal beliefs about our health that sound like vows we have taken. If Molly said it once, she had said it a thousand times: "High blood pressure runs in my family. Both my grandmothers had it and so does my mom, which means I will get it, too." Molly's tribal belief—rooted in fear—was creating a predisposition for illness by lowering her vibration. Her conflict between wanting health and fear of her future drained her energy significantly. Thus her healthy regimes of exercise and organic foods were all but neutralized. Again, the mind, body, and spirit must work together for optimal results. We cannot war within ourselves without paying a price. If you fear a particular illness, it's important to understand the predisposing patterns, your beliefs, and other factors that contribute to that illness. Having this information changes your position from one of fear and powerlessness to one of decisive actions that can change your future.

William feared macular degeneration even though he never

voiced his fears. He watched his dad slowly go blind and couldn't imagine dealing with a similar fate. Even though he never said "It runs in my family," his cells were affected anytime anything to do with sight loss came into William's awareness. Once he became aware of the power of his fear, he made an effort to live fully in the present, where his sight was perfect. By focusing on each day, and not the fear of his future, he stopped a significant energy loss and kept his vibration much higher than before.

Remember that I said that the energy of your thoughts is powerful and it's important to know which ones promote illness, unhappiness, or suffering. Saying that heart disease runs in your family, or your grandfather died young, which means you'll die young, sends a low-vibration message to your cells. Be smart about your health. If two people in your immediate family have diabetes, remember that one of the predispositions for diabetes is losing your dream and feeling trapped. Examine the areas in life where you feel trapped and make new choices, and dare to dream and take a risk. And be smart and don't overload your diet with simple carbohydrates like chips and bread.

If some family members have arthritis (some arthritis comes from being inwardly and quietly self-critical, in a state of generalized worry and fear that wears down the joints), look at the ways you are critical or judgmental of yourself, rewrite your limiting beliefs about safety, forgiveness, and God, and consider some modalities that promote a feeling of safety such as the following:

- Listen to visualization tapes where you are brought to a relaxing and safe place like a calm pond in the woods. (This creates a new cellular memory of comfort rather than panic.)

- Try five to ten minutes of generic meditation daily where you simply repeat a mantra like "one" over and over. (This clears your mind of circling and worrisome thoughts, again creating a new cellular memory of safety and relaxation.)
- Be aware of how you criticize yourself and ask God to help you let such criticisms go.
- Choose each morning to lighten up on yourself for two hours. Even fifteen minutes will help tremendously.
- Wear a blue-based red (it's very grounding and calms you).
- If letting go of your self-criticism feels too hard, consider following a tried-and-true method I am borrowing and revamping from Alcoholics Anonymous: admit that you feel powerless to stop your self-criticism and ask God to help you.

SOME QUESTIONS TO HELP YOU
UNCOVER YOUR TRIBAL BELIEFS

1. Can you imagine healing from your illness?
2. What do you believe you have to do in order to heal?
3. Why wouldn't you heal?

Remember, the mind, body, and spirit all work together under your direction. You are the boss. Healing begins with eliminating the beliefs that thwart your process. It's time to recognize the power of your thoughts and change your thinking.

TRIBAL BELIEFS ABOUT HEALTH AND
HEALING

1. Healing is hard and it takes a long time.
2. If an illness runs in my family, I'll probably get it, too.
3. Don't confront your doctor or give him or her a hard time. Their job is tough enough.
4. Your doctor knows better than you.
5. Let your doctor make the decisions about your treatment.
6. Not everyone deserves to get better.
7. My genes will determine my health, weight, and level of happiness.

Is It Pits or Cherries in the Bowl of Life?

Remember that tribal beliefs seem true—so true, they often become clichés. How many times have you heard *Play the hand you're dealt* or *When life gives you lemons, make lemonade*? Both clichés come from a victim standpoint. They ignore the option of asking for different cards or tossing the lemons in the garbage and going out to buy chocolate instead. Both beliefs share the underlying belief *Life isn't supposed to be easy*. But why not?

Remember when Forrest Gump's mother told him, "Life is like a box of chocolates . . . you never know what you are going to get?" It's true, not everyone has a Magic 8 Ball to predict the future—you don't always know what will happen in life; but you do have a powerful influence and a large say in your future and how you respond to events in your life. One of the reasons I was such a great ER/Trauma nurse is because the busier and hairier the ER became, the more creative I was, the more energized I became, and my abilities to multitask took on a new meaning. Where other nurses would say, "Oh, no, we can't handle another trauma victim," feeling powerless and out of control, I would already have found a free gurney and been setting up for the new patient.

It's all in your attitude and vibration. Yes, it can be stressful and even challenging at times. But you get to decide how you will face those challenges. Consider these tribal beliefs carefully and find the ones that raise your vibration and enjoy them. And get rid of the chocolates with those awful pink creams in them!

QUESTIONS TO HELP YOU UNCOVER YOUR TRIBAL BELIEFS

1. Do you believe people in therapy are weak?
2. Do you find yourself saying, "That's just the way life is" when you meet adversity?
3. Do you judge people who seem to enjoy life too much?
4. What do you believe about people who seem to have it easy in life, about those who easily forgive themselves and move on?
5. What do you think of people who seem to have a lot of happiness in life, or who seem to have everything work out for them?

TRIBAL BELIEFS ABOUT LIFE

1. Life is a struggle.
2. Play the hand you're dealt (you don't realize you can change your hand).
3. When life gives you lemons, make lemonade.
4. There's not enough money/love/good men or women/happiness for everyone.
5. Strong or good people never complain.
6. Struggle in life builds character.
7. You can be proud of continually overcoming adversity—even when you cause it for yourself.
8. You have to keep your promises.
9. Hide your pain—it shows weakness.
10. Confrontation is a bad thing.
11. Risks will only get you hurt.
12. Life is not all about fun—it's work and responsibility, too.
13. In life there are many things you just *have* to do.
14. You have to take life seriously.
15. Life is hard.
16. Always be prepared for the worst.
17. Rewards must be earned.

We have all heard stories of people who came from difficult backgrounds and went on to achieve wonderful things in life, including simply being happy. Look at Luke Skywalker. His father, Darth Vader, went to the dark side. If Luke had the limiting belief *If your father is a bad apple, then you will be a bad apple,* he would have felt powerless to create his destiny. Are you willing to give that much power away, or will you join the ranks of others who are shaping their lives in a manner consistent with their souls? Will you step back from your inheritance and make personal choices about following in your ancestors' footsteps? It's time, and may the Force be with you!

Are People Happy in Disneyworld?

You don't have to visit Disneyworld (the happiest place on Earth) to be happy. The power resides in you to make choices. You've probably seen some very unhappy people in Disneyworld saying, "It's so expensive, it's too crowded, the lines are too long." Yes, perhaps at times this is true, but you knew all that before you went. Now it's up to you to transform the experience. Just like your life—you can hang on to what is wrong with it or focus on what is right with it—that will raise your vibration quickly.

Often I ask a person if being happy is important. "Of course happiness is important. Everyone has the right to be happy" is a frequent response. But people's energies tell me their real truth, even when their mouths don't.

Your tribal beliefs may have taught you that you don't deserve or have the right to be happy, or that being happy isn't a safe or realistic way to live your life. A lot of folks were taught by example in their families that their happiness was not valued or appreciated. With people like this, I encourage them to literally make a decision to be happy. For some it's a simple matter of identifying the tribal belief that says something like *I don't deserve to be happy* or *People like me aren't meant to be happy.* Some of the wonderful rewrites I've seen include:

- It's reasonable to believe that I can change what I was taught I deserve.
- It's reasonable to believe that I can find something that makes me happy.
- It's reasonable to believe that I can choose what tribal beliefs are passed down to me.
- It's reasonable to believe that feeling happy sometimes is good for me.
- It's reasonable to believe that I won't be happy all the time, but sometimes I will.
- It's reasonable to believe that I can be lavished upon and enjoy it (from someone who discovered her goddess energy).
- It's reasonable to believe that I can start making new choices today.

Another big obstacle to happiness arises when people start to become happier than those around them, including their families. It is very tempting to give up your happiness if you have a tribal belief that says *It's not okay to be happy when my family (husband, wife, mother, father, brother, sister) is not.* Before you assume you don't have this particular belief, ask yourself how comfortable you would be becoming a shining light of happiness in your family circle—would you downplay your happiness if you knew your tribe wouldn't celebrate you?

Believe me when I tell you that each tribe has a very specific level of happiness it will allow its members. Some allow a very high level and support their members in achieving it. But more commonly, people run into difficulty when their happiness starts to show. After all, how come you have the right to be so happy when your sister has two autistic children, your cousin has a serious illness, your brother just got laid off, or your dad is in chronic pain from working the job that supported the family while you were growing up? And what gives you the right to be happy when your parents have stuck it out in an unhappy marriage for so many decades? Or how can you be happy when a friend you love is experiencing depression, a breakup or divorce, or is struggling to find his or her way in life?

Please look at all the ways in which you believe you have to give up, silence, or hide your happiness if people you love aren't happy in their lives. If you believe it's not quite okay to shine brightly unless the others you care about are shining just as brightly, you will find ways to sabotage your joy. One woman I worked with found great solace in her rewritten tribal belief: *It's reasonable to believe that everyone I love has the right to choose their level of happiness.* Then she went a step further: *Being happy by shining my brightest inspires others to do the same, if they choose.*

Forrest Gump's mother also taught him that he had to make his own destiny—he was in charge of being happy and fulfilled or not. You have the same rights. So again, I ask you, do you want to make choices in the important arena of happiness based on the authority of people from your past who just happened to be older and taller than you were—and who, by the way, may not have known a single thing about being happy?

SOME QUESTIONS TO HELP YOU
UNCOVER YOUR TRIBAL BELIEFS

1. Do you judge people who seem too happy? As if they don't take anything seriously enough?
2. Are you wary of people who smile all the time?
3. Is it unrealistic to be happy most of the time?

TRIBAL BELIEFS ABOUT HAPPINESS

1. Don't be too happy because something bad is around the corner.
2. Don't get your hopes up because it might not happen.
3. You have to pay for your happiness either up front or at the end.
4. You have to earn your happiness.

Sex, the Chandelier, and the Swinger

Prescribed beliefs about the nature of sexuality can be oppressive and damaging. I've done Readings of many people whose sex lives were unfulfilling because of their tribal beliefs. My Readings show me they are "swing from the chandeliers" adventurous people who would love to enjoy their sexuality, but they mute themselves to fit in their prescribed role—the good girl, the serious husband. And people wonder why they are tired all the time. It takes a tremendous amount of energy to not be who you are.

Devon is a knockout. She could walk into a room in a

sweatshirt, dirty jeans, and sneakers, and her goddess sensuality would light up her outward appearance. She's the kind of beautiful woman about whom the rest of us shake our heads and say, "She's the type who wakes up beautiful!" But Devon's goddess energy could not express herself because of her tribal belief that a woman who dresses attractively or flirts is a slut. The ironic thing is that Devon actually thought her loose turtleneck sweaters and baggy pants somehow hid her inherent sensuality. No way. She would look great in a potato sack!

Devon was expending and wasting a ton of energy trying to hide who she really was, because her church and family taught her that only loose women exuded their femininity. Her beliefs dampened her sex life with her husband and her ability to be free and casual with other people. She hemorrhaged energy trying to keep a lid on her sensuality and safeguard her pure reputation.

After rewriting her tribal belief she emerged glowing, happy, and no longer apologetic about who she was. Her new energetic broadcast—*Flirting with my husband is fun,* and *Acknowledging my beauty is a way of saying thank you to my Higher Power*—changed the way her husband treated her, and they are now very happy together. She thoroughly enjoys her sexuality without a hint of apology.

I met Bill in a workshop. At sixty-seven, he was doing serious manual labor—remodeling his house, landscaping his yard—as well as making time for all of his wife and children's demands. He was exhausted and resentful, a heart attack waiting to happen. His tribal belief was *A good man works hard for his family.* The unspoken tag line of this tribal belief is *If you don't work hard for your family, you aren't a good man.* Now, this may sound like a tribal belief about work, but it's really about gender roles. Bill's motivation was to be a good *man,* a real *man.*

Even though Bill admitted that it would be stupid for a man to work himself into the grave just to be a good man, he continued doing it. Even though he knew that other qualities defined a good man, he continued his physical labor. His conflict was simple. His father had taught him *A good man works until he dies.* Only when Bill suffered a heart attack did he sheepishly choose to rewrite his tribal belief regarding the definition of a good man.

In many cultures, men are expected to be tough, aggressive, and more doers than feelers. Along comes Gary, who is sensitive and quiet. Suddenly his testosterone level is scrutinized by others in the tribe. Gary doesn't care for football, likes a woman on equal footing, and craves beauty in the world. The other men in his tribe have doubts about Gary because he doesn't fit the tribal mold that says *Real men love contact sports, Real men are in charge of their women,* and *Real men are strong, not sensitive.*

Poor Gary breaks tribal laws just by waking up in the morning and appreciating the sunrise. His father and brothers wonder about him constantly. They often attempt to bring him into the fold and get frustrated at his lame attempts to enjoy sports. Gary's conflict—feeling like he didn't belong—became so overwhelming that he stopped visiting his brothers.

"I just couldn't stand feeling like there was something wrong with me all the time," he said. "So I went out to find people like me."

Gary's journey to acceptance was what saved him. He not only found many men who were like him, but many women who liked him just the way he was. In fact, he found out that his sensitive nature contributed to his reputation as a good catch. And he enjoys every moment of it!

Gary is a fine example of someone choosing to look beyond the prison walls of the tribe, entertain alternative possibilities, and take charge of his life. He stopped investing his energy in trying to fit in with a tribe whose taunts became too much to bear. Gary found peace rather quickly.

SOME QUESTIONS TO HELP YOU UNCOVER YOUR TRIBAL BELIEFS

1. What's your opinion of women who choose a career over having children?
2. How do you feel around husbands or wives who "roll over" for their spouse?
3. What are the characteristics of an ideal man? Woman?

TRIBAL BELIEFS ABOUT SEXUALITY AND GENDER ROLES

1. Only cheap, easy, or promiscuous women flirt or dress sensuously.
2. Blondes are dumb.
3. Only bad girls or sluts enjoy sex.

4. Men are made differently—you can't always expect them to be monogamous.

5. Powerful women aren't feminine.

6. Being sensitive is not manly.

7. Homosexuality is a choice some people make.

8. It's the woman's fault for getting pregnant.

9. A good husband makes more money than his wife.

10. Women who choose not to have children are incomplete and not real women.

11. A woman should defer to her husband's needs.

12. It's a woman's job to take care of the house.

13. If a woman gets emotional, she must be on her period.

14. If a woman is aggressive, she's probably a lesbian and dislikes men.

15. The family business should go to the son, not the daughter.

16. Real men don't cry, it's a sign of weakness.

17. A good woman stands behind her man.

18. Women are too emotional.

19. Never outshine your husband.

To Whom Much Is Given, Much Is Required

As you can imagine, God is a topic that can polarize a room in seconds. Try to remember that in most cases, your beliefs about God (until you rewrite them) are ruled by your family's tribal beliefs, the teachings of your religion, and the belief system or culture of the section of the country you grew up in. You might even have learned two diametrically opposing beliefs regarding God—*Fear the vengeful God* and *Embrace the loving and forgiving God.* I have watched people defend their positions on God with deep emotion, only to find in the end they did not believe what they were saying. They were merely repeating what their tribe had taught them.

I often teach people how to access their guidance and ask God for help to make their lives easier. Frequently people's fear of asking help from God is overpowering. Their belief that God is just waiting for them to screw up and smite them is chilling. The belief that their suffering is because God is punishing them is sad. To people like this, every bump in the road is a punishment from God. During the fateful Katrina and Rita hurricanes in the autumn of 2005, some preachers announced publicly that the hurricanes were God's way of exacting vengeance on sinners. I shudder to think of all the innocents who believed those statements and were hurt by them.

Nancy is a big-hearted and big-spirited woman who got pregnant without being married. Because she believed that *God is vengeful and punishes sinners,* she lived her entire life trying to make amends to a God she feared, convincing herself she was not a good person. When she lost her job, it was because God was punishing her. When her child became sick, it was God exacting retribution. When she developed breast cancer, it was God wanting her to suffer. The impact of Nancy's tribal beliefs about God was traumatic and unnecessary.

Each time adversity struck, Nancy shouldered the suffering alone. She would not dare ask God for help, solace, or guidance.

Thinking she deserved punishment, she never asked her friends for help. She definitely didn't ask her family of origin for support, because they were the ones who had taught her she was suffering because of her sins. In their world, there was no forgiveness for mistakes. Nancy lived a tortured existence in perpetual fear, in hatred of herself, and alone without any connection to her spirit. She also died without redemption.

Livia was a proud, strong, and intelligent woman who tackled tough projects in life. She took care of unwanted children in the inner city. Yet, she was terrified of God. Her tribal beliefs dictated:

- God is vengeful and out to hurt me.
- God will never answer a prayer for something I can do myself.
- Asking God for help will only get me in trouble.

When Livia became ill, she refused—no, demanded—that no one pray for her. She did not want to be on God's radar. She was so certain that God wanted to punish her for all of her wrongdoings that she never prayed or asked for help. She lived a lifetime of long-term suffering and fear, believing that God wanted to hurt her.

Livia's pride was so strong, she refused to entertain the idea of looking at her tribal beliefs. Naturally, she also had the tribal belief *Suffering is noble*—so the more, the better. "Bring it on!" was her motto. To her, the more trials she had, the more character she built.

When I did a Reading on Livia, I saw that she had a lot of energy invested in her belief that God was out to punish her. But the return on her investment was poor—she lived in fear and refused any help from the spiritual realm. She blamed God for her misfortunes, an approach that guarantees the status quo—she wouldn't consider changing her life because her misfortune is God's fault, not hers.

"I thought you were tough," I said. "I didn't know you were actually a weakling. Blaming God for your troubles is another way of saying you are a powerless victim, with no say in life. Is this what you teach the unwanted inner-city kids—that their lot in life is a punishment from God?"

Boy, did I ever have her attention. Livia looked like she might explode and then burst out laughing. "You *are* good. Okay, you got me and you're right. It is being weak to blame someone else for your problems. What do I need to do?"

I can't think of any sweeter words than those. She rewrote her tribal belief about God and asked me to pray with her. This moment is one of the richest rewards I receive through my work—helping people to connect with God and learn to trust their guidance.

You are in charge of whether you are forgiven or not.

I always ask my clients to look deeply at their beliefs about God. I can't even begin to ascertain where all these negative beliefs came from, but they abound. I can promise you that any belief that you hold about a Higher Power not being behind you 100 percent is damaging to your energy system. And for those of you who don't believe in God or a Higher Power, all I can say is that this shows when I Read your energetic blueprint. Now, I'm not saying you have to believe a certain way. Not at all. I'm just saying that I can always see the negative effect on someone's energy system when they feel spiritually disconnected or alone. It's like a wise woman, who was over one hundred at the time, once told me: "I can always tell when someone has God in their life," she said. "There's a light on inside them."

SOME QUESTIONS TO HELP YOU UNCOVER YOUR TRIBAL BELIEFS

1. Do you believe that adversity in life is a punishment?
2. Does being spiritual require certain sacrifices?
3. Is it God's will when a child dies?

TRIBAL BELIEFS ABOUT GOD AND SPIRITUALITY

1. God will only love me if I am good.
2. People who believe in God are weak—they do not face reality or handle life on their own.
3. Never bother God, saints, or angels with small things. There are too many big problems in the world that need their help.

4. If I believe in God, I am giving my power away.

5. If I ask God for guidance, I'll be told to do something I don't want to, like be a missionary, go live in poverty, or open a soup kitchen for the homeless.

6. Be wary of God—His wrath is terrible.

7. Enlightened people do not judge others and have total self-acceptance.

8. Spirituality requires a measure of abstinence, suffering, or denial of one's self.

9. Spiritual people must sacrifice or pull back from the material world into a world of celibacy, quiet, and hard work.

10. Spiritual people rarely make mistakes.

11. Spiritual people don't get angry and have no worldly desires.

12. My problems are small, and it's not right to ask God for help when there are people worse off than me who really need the help.

13. Asking God for help means I'm weak.

14. If I ask God for help and get it, I will owe something, and I don't like the feeling of owing something.

15. If I struggle through on my own, it builds character.

16. Asking for help is embarrassing. It implies I'm a failure.

17. I thought only spiritual or good people received help.

18. I don't know the right way to ask God for help.
19. God never answers my prayers. He's only supposed to listen to them.

I Was Hurt Too Badly to Get Over It

A painful childhood is cruel enough, but imagine extending that childhood into your eighties. People who have tribal beliefs about their childhood wounds suffer for a long, long time. They identify themselves through their wounds, and they bond with each other based on their wounds. Every retreat I have taught shows me the power of wounds kept alive because of a tribal belief. If there are four people with unhealed childhood wounds in a retreat of forty people, they will find one another across the crowded room and bond based on a litany of their hurts. They tend to exclude people with happy childhoods because they simply cannot understand a life without wounding.

I have seen adults wounded in childhood spend a considerable amount of time either lamenting or being angry about their past. I often hear them wishing life had been different for them. All too frequently, I hear a devastating remark about their old pain: "I will never get over it."

Don't program your cells to be in perpetual pain. Don't insist on keeping your wounds active and bleeding. Do consider that your loyalty to your wounds is based on a tribal belief that simply is not in alignment with your soul. All your soul wants is for you to heal and be happy.

SOME QUESTIONS TO HELP YOU UNCOVER YOUR TRIBAL BELIEFS

1. Do you believe that childhood wounds leave such permanent damage that you can never have a normal life?
2. Do you believe that you must understand or remember everything that happened to you in order to heal it?
3. Do you think that your childhood wounds explain why your life isn't going the way you want it to?

TRIBAL BELIEFS ABOUT CHILDHOOD WOUNDS

1. If you didn't get what you needed as a child, you'll never get it.
2. You never fully recover from the bad things that happened when you were a child.
3. No one understands what you went through.
4. It takes a long time to get over it.
5. Your wounds will always haunt you.
6. You were powerless then, and you're powerless now.
7. The aftereffects of your childhood wounds will be with you for the rest of your life.
8. Childhood sexual abuse affects a person's whole life.
9. If God lets you be hurt as a kid, he doesn't really love you.
10. People will continue to get away with screwing you over for the rest of your life.

Very often, a person who has experienced childhood wounding is angry with God, believing that God had abandoned or punished them. This belief carries over into adulthood, leaving them with little self-esteem or source for comfort.

If you have experienced childhood wounding, it is important to recognize the warping effect it will have on your connection to and beliefs about God. I suggest working on these two tribal areas simultaneously for the greatest benefit.

Caution: Funeral Ahead—No Smiling

I met Kay, a sixty-two-year-old woman who had lost her husband years earlier. From January to October, she was a globe-hopping jet-setter, but come November, everything changed. Her attire turned to black and dark blues, and she spent a lot of time kneeling in the Greek Orthodox Church and mourning her husband. Kay believed that if you forgot your loved one at the holidays, you were slime. She believed that holidays were the time to remember she was alone and mourn. She could not possibly enjoy the remaining members of her family. She had to feel badly about being alone; it showed how much she cared for her late husband. Kay held ceremonies at the church and big productions to honor him. The community saw how she honored her late husband and approved. She was one with the tribe, until the following January when she put on brightly colored clothes and went off to enjoy life again.

Tribes evolve when individuals take risks.

Kay's tribal belief was so strong it ruined her holidays and scared the rest of the family into being respectful and feeling (or acting) sad during them. Kay's inner clock ran without her conscious input. It has been over eleven years and she still wears black starting in November and arranges memorials for her late husband, extolling his virtues to the rest of the congregation. I often wonder how much she dreads holidays.

In contrast, I had the pleasure of working with a dynamic woman in her sixties who became radiantly beautiful through the inner work she was willing to do. In fact, the rumor swirling around her town was that she'd "had a little work done." She had, but not the kind they thought! After losing her husband fifteen years ago, Jennance's tribal beliefs dictated that her love life was over. But her spirit wanted so much more. So she started working on the tribal beliefs that say *You are lucky to have one good marriage, you cannot expect another, A grandmother does not fall in love,* and *It dishonors the memory of your mate to fall in love again.*

All I can say is, "Wow!" What a role model! Jennance's natural elegance and power radiated from her. She now only dates men who raise her vibration and enjoys her social life immensely. Her children (all eight of them) were astounded at the changes in their mother. You see, Jennance also changed her energetic broadcast. She no longer sent out the message that she had to sacrifice herself for her children to be a good mother.

She grew to really love and respect herself, and she effortlessly commanded newfound respect and appreciation from her tribe. Most of all, her grandchildren noticed the change in Nana. Can you imagine the powerful new tribal beliefs she is passing on, not only to her grown children, but to her grandchildren as well? This is how tribes evolve: thanks to individuals who are willing to take the risk and let their souls shine.

Her last note reported "Love has come sweeping into my life." I can't wait to meet the man lucky enough to be with her.

On the East Coast, wakes and elaborate funerals are routine. On the West Coast, it seems more common to have a simple memorial service. One thing I have noticed is that these rituals are quite somber in certain tribes and more lighthearted in others. Grief is often the way people honor the dead—they believe grieving means that you cared for that person. They also believe that if you are not in excruciating pain about losing someone, you did not really love them. The disparity in people's expressions of grief is a testament to the power of cultural tribal beliefs. I have learned from crossing over with some of my clients that when someone dies, they go to a place of exquisite peace and joy.

Donna lost someone important to her—her father. A friend bought her a flower that only blooms once a year—to commemorate the one-year anniversary of his passing. We have all heard how that first-year anniversary is the hardest, and that tribal belief was being programmed into her cells, heart, and mind. She was expected to feel terrible at the one-year mark—and the blooming orchid would remind her to feel appropriately. Can you imagine if Donna felt good on that day? She might consider herself abnormal.

I did a Reading for thirty-nine-year-old Alice, who had lost her husband five years earlier. She told me how devastated she was to lose him and felt like her life was in shambles, and she was simply going through the motions each day, devoid of any joy or laughter.

My Reading showed a woman in tremendous conflict. A powerful tribal belief was literally shutting down her life. Alice had the tribal belief *A good woman remains faithful to her dead husband—whether she is twenty-three or sixty-three.* Remaining alone showed the world that she was a good woman who loved her husband. Although I introduced her to people who would support her healing process, when invited out to the theater, for coffee, or for a walk, she always declined. She thought it was wrong to enjoy herself—after all, she was a widow. This was a powerful tribal belief that she would not even consider rewriting.

My energy assessment revealed that her words were hollow and not how she really felt at all. The truth was, she could not stand her husband and was secretly glad he was dead. She endured an emotionally lonely life because her other tribal belief was *Marriage is forever.* Period.

Her energy blueprint revealed her internal conflict—she was relieved to be liberated from him but needed to maintain the tribal standard of the grieving widow. Alice's other secret was out. She felt like a horrible person for feeling happy.

Alice had trouble examining her tribal beliefs because for

her, things were black or white: she was a good woman or not. Her reputation was so important to her, she would not stray from the rules. This decision cost her dearly.

She remains locked in a conflicted and unhappy state. Alice reminds me of the elephants kept in a circus. Attached to a post, a very short chain is tied around the elephant's leg. After this bondage creates a cellular memory in the elephant, the chain can be removed, but the elephant will not run away—it believes it is still trapped. The chains around Alice had been removed, but she was too scared and bound by her limiting beliefs to walk away to freedom.

SOME QUESTIONS TO HELP YOU UNCOVER YOUR TRIBAL BELIEFS

1. What do you think about people who recover from loss relatively quickly?
2. Is there an appropriate amount of time one should grieve a loved one's death?
3. Do you think it's okay to be dishonest in a eulogy?

TRIBAL BELIEFS ABOUT GRIEVING

1. It's inappropriate to have fun or happy moments when someone you care about is dying.
2. You cannot get over someone's death or go back to enjoying life too soon because it shows you did not truly care about them.
3. You shouldn't put energy into taking care of your own needs when someone you care about is very ill or dying.

4. To mourn someone is to honor them.
5. You can only say nice things about people once they die.
6. The amount of pain you feel for someone who has died is commensurate with the love you had for them.
7. It is appropriate to feel sadness or grief as the anniversary of a loved one's death approaches.

By now you've learned a lot about your unconscious. It's time to start rewriting the limiting beliefs you no longer need. But let's address some of the most common objections to letting go of limiting tribal beliefs.

7.

"Alex, I'd Like to Buy a New Tribal Belief for One Hundred, Please"

ARE YOU IN CHARGE OF YOUR LIFE AND
LOYAL TO YOUR SPIRIT?

When confronted with one of their toxic tribal beliefs, people will either defend it loyally or judge it. They will call the belief stupid and swear they would not follow it. In further conversation, they usually discover that they are following that "stupid" tribal belief quite loyally. At this point they may get stuck in their anger at the stupidity of the belief and their willingness to remain true to it, or they may become sad and even depressed that they wasted their valuable time following it.

Mary was depressed but willing to be sick to stay loyal to

her beliefs. Diagnosed with fibromyalgia, Mary told me she wanted to heal. Over the years, I have found that people with fibromyalgia have the precursor of not enjoying life. Several tribal beliefs feed that energetic predisposition:

- Keep your nose to the grindstone.
- Life isn't meant to be enjoyed.
- Hard work makes you a good person, and enjoying yourself is akin to laziness.
- Don't be selfish—take care of commitments, children, or other people before yourself.
- It is not okay to be happy when the rest of your family is not.
- Being too happy can easily lead to being irresponsible.
- If you have made mistakes in life, you must always pay for them by denying some of your happiness and pleasure.

When I explained to Mary that she carried the tribal belief that she did not deserve pleasure in her life and that it stood in the way of her healing, she responded, "I do indeed believe I deserve pleasure!" This was her rational mind speaking to me. In the course of our conversation, however, Mary revealed she had a long history of hard work at difficult jobs, she'd been in a string of relationships that started well but ended in abysmal breakups, and she had not taken a vacation in over twenty years. Her last time off was used to move across the country.

When I tried to show her how these events related to her tribal belief that she was not supposed to enjoy life, Mary could not see any connection. She refused to acknowledge the possibility of a conflict within her. Working hard was simply the right thing to do! I was stunned at her willingness to attribute these hardships to "the way life is," rather than to her tribal beliefs. It was simply another way of saying, "I'm choosing to be loyal to my tribe rather than my spirit."

Mary insisted her life was difficult because of unforeseen and uncontrollable events. She later defended her position by saying, "I couldn't take a vacation, we were too busy at work." She could not see that her beliefs helped to create these events by her personal choices. She had clearly made two significant choices: no vacation and relationships that were way more work than fun.

The truth was that she was in conflict with her soul. Mary felt that not working would suggest to her family and friends that she was lazy. She desperately wanted approval from each of them. Although she was exhausted and said she would love to lie on a beach for a week and do nothing but sleep, her desire to please her family overwhelmed her good sense. She had mixed feelings about where to place her loyalty. Moreover, she valued other people's opinion of her and did not want to be known as lazy or unproductive. According to Mary's tribal beliefs, taking a vacation meant exactly that. Asking her to take a vacation and give her body a rest was akin to blasphemy.

Because of her strong attachment to her tribal belief *Hard work makes you a good person*, pleasure in life remained a distant and unimportant goal for Mary. She still suffers with fibromyalgia because her pride wouldn't let her admit there was a connection between her pain, her difficult circumstances, and her beliefs.

Nor could she concede that her tribal belief was not serving her highest good and she had the power to change it if she wanted to. But she could admit that she was afraid to be disloyal to her family's value and was concerned for her reputation. Can you see from Mary's situation that many tribal beliefs are rooted in fear?

Our spirit is always urging us forward, toward spiritual enrichment, toward happiness, and into a passionate life. Our spirit guides us toward a high vibration. From time to time, there will be conflict with one of your tribal beliefs. You may hold on to your old belief from fear of being thought selfish or from guilt, pride, or misplaced loyalty. All of these can block your way to freedom and joy. The question is, when your soul speaks, what will it take to make you listen and change the tribal belief that is keeping you—and eventually your children and others you influence—from the happiness that is your birthright?

Misplaced and Mistaken Loyalty

How far will people go to stay loyal to their tribal beliefs? Sadly, some people will actually die for them—physically, emotionally, or spiritually. Balance is the key to good health, and that requires the nurturing of your mind, body, and spirit. So although you can live with the pain of a lonely relationship or an oppressive job, it requires you to ignore and wall off a part of you that will eventually wither and die. Emotionally dead or spiritually bereft, many individuals walk through the motions of life because they are not willing to think outside their tribe.

Are these the reasons you will dishonor and abuse the sacred gift of life by not living it fully and according to the guidance of your spirit?

- To please your family by adhering to their rules?
- To stay true to tribal laws because that's all you know and what you were taught?
- Because you are scared of trying something new and stepping out on your own?

Are these valid reasons for your loyalty—your loyalty that deprives your spirit of life? I sit with people who have lost the use of their legs and yearn to run, or lost their sight and crave color. Many choices have been taken from them, yet they choose to be happy. When I watch you choose to stay loyal to a belief that paralyzes your spirit, I weep.

Alicia was a thirty-one-year-old with a zest for life. Not married, she was happy as a clam. She had a great social life, enjoyed her alone time, and focused on her career as a graphic designer. Her tribe members, however, were relentless. They wanted her to marry—their tribal law was not flattering to women who did not marry. When Alicia finally caved in to tribal belief pressure and married, her family was thrilled. They had worried that she wasn't "the marrying type" and knew that wouldn't look good in the community.

At thirty-two, Alicia married a handsome and gregarious man who changed within a year of marriage. He emotionally abused her with derogatory comments and criticisms, which progressed to awful name-calling. A three-day barrage of apologies, gifts, and an apparently reformed and loving attitude followed each tirade.

Alicia continued to smile and act happy on the outside, but when I Read her energetic blueprint, I found a trapped and dying young woman. She had started to have symptoms—fatigue, joint pains, inability to tolerate sunlight, rashes, and a general feeling of sickness. I saw that the energetic predisposition for lupus was swirling around her, and it was progressing fast.

Alicia was adamant that she could not leave her marriage. She believed:

- Marriage is sacred and forever no matter what.
- You cannot leave a marriage unless you have tried *everything* to save the marriage (so if a spouse refuses to try marriage counseling—as her husband had—you have not tried everything).
- People who get divorced are failures.
- If you get divorced, you stain the family reputation.

In Alicia's tribe, divorce was a heinous crime. Good people just did not do it. Even when Alicia tried to tell her family about the abuse, her mother explained that men will be men and Alicia just needed to try harder. Besides, he was always nice when around the family, so apparently Alicia must be doing something to anger him.

Trapped, without the support of her tribe, Alicia had to make a choice to heal an emotional and now physical issue or die. Her fear of breaking tribal law was so great—they would ridicule and disown her—that she continued to try to make the marriage work. Her choice to ignore her spirit, which screamed for her to leave the marriage, was her undoing. When Alicia was diagnosed with lupus the following year, her husband left her. She returned to live with her family. Her disgrace at being left ate at her daily; she was bedridden within six months. She never could forgive herself for the breakup of her marriage.

I have also done many Readings for men and women who are unhappily married to very nice spouses. They believe *You shouldn't leave a nice person* and *You don't divorce a good person because a good man or woman is hard to find.* When these beliefs are in conflict with your soul, do they deserve your loyalty?

Five Steps to Recognize a Tribal Belief Causing You Conflict

I. **Notice the emotional warning signs of a limiting tribal belief:**
   - Feeling frustrated or trapped like you have no choices
   - Feeling resentful that you have to do something
   - Feeling tired from playing mental Ping-Pong between what you want to do versus what you are supposed to do
   - Feeling guilty
   - Be willing to admit your spirit is in conflict with your tribe

2. **Put into words exactly what you think you should be doing.**

3. **Explain why you should be doing it.** The "why" will give you a good idea of what your tribal belief is. Try to find the exact right words to express it: when you write or speak the limiting belief, it may exacerbate the feelings above.

4. **Ask yourself, if there were no logistical considerations, what would you *really* want to do?** The answer to this question gets you past all your excuses: if no one was hurt by your actions, no one became angry at you, and everyone supported your decision, what would you do? This is where your spirit gets a voice. Let's start off with an easy question. What do you really want to do when you receive a holiday fruitcake? Do you wait for it to turn rock hard on your counter before throwing it away—because of your limiting belief about gifts—or do you give it to someone who actually likes fruitcake?

5. **Does your answer energize or drain you?** Sit in a quiet place and talk to your spirit—not your mind—and I promise you will get a very clear answer. Ask yourself, does it raise or lower your vibration? Does it make you happier? Does it contribute to your spiritual evolution or slow it down? The answer is either yes or no. There are no mental gymnastics involved. Either the answer does or it does not. If your answer does not energize,

excite you, or raise you up, then you are still operating under a limiting tribal belief. This is an important choice point for you.

> *Your spirit's recommendations will always raise your vibration.*

Listen to your spirit, even if it disagrees with what you were taught. Your spirit's recommendations will always raise your vibration. You are moments away from making a sacred choice that will change your life for the better.

Guidelines for Rewriting Your Limiting Tribal Beliefs

If your new choice makes you happier but you still feel some guilt as if you are doing something wrong, it's time to rewrite your belief. Rewriting tribal beliefs is an easy but extremely honest process. When you are ready to change your life for the better, here are some guidelines to help you:

I. Don't rewrite a tribal belief by simply saying the opposite. For example, *Suffering makes me a better person* cannot be rewritten as *Suffering does not make me a better person,* because you simply won't believe it. You've carried your limiting beliefs for a long time and there's a lot of loyalty tied up in them. You need an incremental approach.

2. Always begin your rewrite with, "It is reasonable to believe . . ." This allows your mind to consider the possibility and gradually change. It is a gentler approach, and one your mind is more likely to accept.

3. Think outside of your proverbial box. For example, *A good mother is responsible for her child's happiness* can be rewritten as *It is reasonable to believe that loving mothers sometimes raise children who choose to be unhappy.*

4. When you find a limiting belief, look at how it plays out in your daily life. What does it look like? What choices and decisions are you making (or not making) based on it? What problems is it preventing you from solving? How is it making you behave? (It's helpful to do this exploration in writing.) For example, do you choose to work late rather than go to the gym because a good husband or father thinks of his family before himself, or are you staying in a relationship that drains you because of a limiting belief about long-term friendships?

   Remember two points at this stage:

   • As you note how the limiting belief plays out in your life, remember to look for the subtle ways you stay loyal. Depending on your total blueprint (such as archetypal makeup, traumas, etc.), you may follow the rules in a less than obvious way. It's time for you to play detective and see all the facts.

- You may get rather sophisticated at telling yourself you have changed a limiting belief when you haven't. For example, you will tell me, "I don't hang out with anyone who is negative and brings me down." Except when I look in your energy field, I see a draining relationship that is the reason for your recent fatigue. When I ask how come, you reply, "It's because my friend is sick (the limiting belief *You don't kick someone when they are down*). You have made an exception and the drain is not because the friend is sick, but because she is negative, complains all the time, and is punitive toward her visitors. The true drain is that you feel you can't stop visiting her.

  Or when you tell me you don't work late at the office, but I see you go home and feel guilty and thus clean the garage, hang a door, and work around the house, I know you are simply following the tribal belief *A good person works hard* in a subtle and sophisticated way.

5. Look at how that belief has played out in years past. I want you to really *get* how big an effect the tribal belief is having on your life. Rewrite your tribal belief or let it go. Many people find that rewriting their belief is the most effective way to

change it. If you do this, work on your rewrite until it really clicks, until it really feels right. Ask yourself, what would I rather believe instead? Then spend some time and find exactly the right words that you can feel in your body.

6. As you do the rewriting process, you will need to brainstorm some ideas. Get together with some open-minded friends and see what develops. The good news is that the Truth really does set us free, and like the wind, you may not always see Truth, but you will always feel it. That feeling is the cha-ching effect (see the next section).

    Write down your new belief and practice it. If your new belief says *It is reasonable to take care of myself while I take care of others*, then set up a gym schedule for yourself.

7. Say your new belief aloud several times a day for two weeks. You can even write out new beliefs and put them on your mirror in the bathroom. Get comfortable with the new you.

8. Create a Tribal Log and record your progress. Your log contains

    • The original limiting belief.

    • One or two specific ways it has affected your de-cisions, problem-solving abilities, and choices.

    • The new rewrite. This rewrite may be honed and modified the more comfortable you become with it.

    • One or two new actions that reflect your new tribal belief.

- One way you have celebrated your newfound freedom and integrity of spirit.

A Tribal Log is a powerful tool to monitor your progress, but it can also be a tremendous gift to your children. Remember that you are passing down a tribal inheritance—conscious and unconscious. Your children will thank you for your honesty, bravery, and willingness to create an easier life for your family.

The Cha-Ching Effect

Please stand before a mirror and while watching yourself, say something utterly and very untrue, and notice how it feels. Then say something you would stake your life on, and feel the difference in your body. That is the "cha-ching," a kinesthetic response initiated by the cells of your body celebrating. Your spirit adds the wonderful tingling and goose bumps that follow.

The cha-ching effect is like an energetic lie detector. I see when your statements dissipate in your energy field, leaving no energetic signature. This means that I can tell when people are not being truthful, even if it's a lie they believe.

CHA-CHING EFFECT

A moment of profound knowing as you feel Truth vibrate through your body.

When you pay attention, you will feel the cha-ching effect in your body and recognize the lack of it in others. It is a powerful tool for discovering your truth.

I often give this example when teaching. I stand before the audience and ask the group to pay attention to my energetic broadcast.

My first statement, "I like brussels sprouts," causes the room to erupt in laughter. My throat becomes constricted, my voice quite deep, and the cells in my body react as though I said I was going to dunk myself in the Ganges River. This is because I hate brussels sprouts. The audience has no trouble reading my energy.

My next statement is "I like deep, rich, Dove dark chocolate." The energy is completely different; the cha-ching effect is unmistakable, as the chocolate-loving energy runs through me. My cells literally quiver with anticipation. Often after the lunch break I find a bar of dark chocolate on my seat!

Remember, when you rewrite a tribal belief, it isn't something you are forcing yourself to believe. When the words are right for you, there will be an ease and a little excitement as you say them. The idea, while new, feels possible.

> *You cannot stay in your head and change your vibration.*

You are opening your mind a little, the amount you can comfortably tolerate. It's important that you have at least a little response in your body that tells you this new way of thinking makes sense to you, or at least maybe could be true. Other ways that people have described this feeling are: "The words just clicked; I felt a little excitement; it felt right; my words made me calm and happy; I just knew the words were right."

This experience can happen instantaneously and feel like a perfect fit (like me and chocolate), or it can take minutes or even days as the impact of your new beliefs unfolds before you. Give those new beliefs a chance if they feel good, even if you still are not completely convinced. They will morph into what is right for you and then you'll feel that shiver of excitement. Don't worry, you'll know when a statement isn't right for you; it will feel flat or like simple head chatter.

If a new tribal belief (or affirmation) stays only in your head, saying it a million times will not change your energy as much as saying a statement you can feel in your body once. In other words, you cannot stay in your head and change your vibration. You must combine your mind, body, and spirit to change your energetic blueprint.

Your mind will think of the new tribal belief, your body will feel it, and your spirit will advise you.

A client once told me, "Only stupid people pray to God for help. Smart people help themselves." The result of this tribal belief was that she struggled constantly with her fears and her separation from God. So I suggested a rewrite that would feel true to her without overwhelming her. I didn't try to get her to believe that asking for help was smart. That was too big a step. I simply asked her if it was reasonable to consider asking for help once in a while. She thought it over and said yes. I watched as the tears fell slowly down her cheeks as she thought about my words. "It really is okay to ask for help, isn't it?" she whispered. She was having a moment of excitement and awe as she spoke her new tribal belief, *It is reasonable to ask God for help now and again.* Her cha-ching effect changed her life. As time goes by and she grows comfortable with her new way of living, I expect she will revise this belief even more.

Now let's follow George as he identifies and rewrites a limiting tribal belief. George wanted to be financially independent. He had spent nearly $70,000 on seminars by famous people about the ins and outs of making money. He had a panoply of spreadsheets and binders guiding him in his quest for financial freedom. But after three years of trying all of the techniques he'd learned, he was no closer to his goal.

George came to one of my seminars wanting answers. His wife, Shirley, nearly had to drag him because my seminar description did not mention financial freedom. "But Christel will know why nothing has worked," she promised him. Shirley knew that at all of my events, I do Readings of energetically receptive attendees, and she was betting that the answer George was seeking was in his energetic blueprint, not in any $10,000 manual.

So George came—and he brought his spreadsheets—

determined to find out the reason he was failing miserably. After two hours, George raised his hand and finally asked, "Why can't I make any money?" He knew something was not working in his life and was ready to consider the possibility that there were alternatives to the way he had been taught to make money.

I welcomed George's question as it gave me an opportunity to teach the group about tribal beliefs. It didn't matter whether the issue was relationships, sex, God, health, or money. I quickly scanned George and saw the answer. I also knew he wasn't going to like it and would fight me on it.

"I have one question for you," I said, noticing that Shirley was listening eagerly. "First, did those courses teach you that it is easy to make money? That you don't have to work hard for it?"

"Absolutely," George responded proudly. "That's the whole idea. You don't have to work hard at all! I don't want to be one of those people who works hard his whole life just to earn some money."

"But the problem is," I answered quietly, "you *are* one of those people."

George sputtered and turned red, highly insulted. "I spent thousands of dollars—" he began.

"Yes," I interrupted, "and you are no closer to your goal. If you would like to find out why, try listening."

George was almost to his feet when Shirley snatched him back into his chair and gave him a look that could have quelled an angry bear. George sank quietly into his seat and glared at me.

I explained to the group about tribal beliefs regarding

money and asked George if I could use him as an example. He agreed. I told him I had seen a tribal belief in him: *Money earned without hard work is tainted money. It's like ill-gotten gains.* George didn't know it, but I was identifying which tribal belief was blocking his way.

Taken aback, George nodded. Deeply Christian, he had learned that good money came from honest work and that working hard was the right way to earn money.

"So, George," I continued, "if your belief system, which now rules you, insists that any money you earn from your new financial ventures is tainted, do you see a conflict inside of you? Part of you wants to make money easily but part of you feels it's wrong. Can you see why your financial dreams have not come true?"

George's wife nearly fell out of her seat with excitement. "I get it!" she shouted. "I get it!" George, however, had not. His logical mind had examined what he'd been taught in all those financial seminars and concluded the principles were sound. His logical mind felt that following those teachings to the letter would produce the results he craved. And they would have, except for his tribal belief, which neutralized all his efforts.

"George, you are broadcasting the energetic message that if you make money easily, you aren't a good Christian." Now I had his attention. It was a powerful conflict.

Of course, being a logical thinker, George wanted to analyze and understand everything I was saying to him. I stopped him cold. "Do you really want to waste more time, or do you want results?" That got him.

I asked him to be quiet and listen to the voice of his spirit. "Is easy money truly tainted? Are you less of a Christian if you make money easily?" George was now listening to his spirit and considering changing his belief. The problem, however, was that George didn't want to believe his life could change so fast and easily.

Letting go of his pride took most of the afternoon. George simply refused to admit that he had wasted all that money and time on all those seminars. He insisted he simply wasn't working the program as efficiently as he could and was certain the problem lay with his efforts, not in his thinking. Getting stuck in his pride consumed George, and for a while all learning ceased. Shirley looked like she might strangle him. Finally, he relented.

Next, when George was ready, I walked him through rewriting his tribal belief. I told him always to begin with the phrase "It is reasonable to believe . . ." because you must start the rewriting process by choosing something that feels reasonable, or at least a little believable to you.

Here is how George rewrote his tribal belief. He started with the tribal belief that was causing him conflict: *Money earned easily is tainted money.* Then he asked himself, "Does it raise or lower my vibration to adhere to this tribal belief?" George was quite clear that working very hard for money did not raise his vibration! Next he took note of how his old tribal belief affected his life. He saw that he had manifested that belief by losing thousands on real estate deals that should have made him money. Shirley added that every money decision George made was onerous and difficult because he had to think it over, weigh the pros and cons, and create more spreadsheets! This allowed him to work hard for the money.

The crucial moment for George had arrived. It was time to decide if he was ready to change the tribal belief. But George had one more objection up his sleeve. He was not ready to change his tribal belief because he thought the process was *too easy*! Fortunately, Shirley was prepared for this and gently prodded him to begin his rewrite. Actually, it was more than gentle prodding!

George began, "It is reasonable. . . ." At his side, Shirley was quietly rewriting the tribal belief while George struggled. George had run into another tribal belief, *Change is hard.* Fortunately, Shirley did not share that one, either, and she went on to help him rewrite both old beliefs. With each proposed rewrite, George checked inside for what I call the cha-ching effect, the feeling that the new belief really clicks with you, that it is truly in alignment with your soul. Here's what he came up with:

1. It's reasonable to believe that consulting with God, not just spreadsheets, makes my financial decisions much easier.
2. It's reasonable to believe that working hard is not an effective way to decontaminate the money I earn.
3. It's reasonable to believe that sometimes change is hard, but not always. It's reasonable to believe that not all change is hard.

Now it was time for George to trust his guidance. I asked him to pray for help during the break. He returned to class bewildered but excited. "I got an answer," he said sheepishly. "I know what I need to do."

George left the workshop a changed man. He threw away all the manuals and training guides, sold his remaining real estate, moved to his dream location, and wrote a book. He thoroughly enjoyed the writing process, and to hear him tell it, it was quite easy. I doubt that he'll have any problem with the money he earns.

It's time to take an inventory of what you own: the beliefs, values, criticisms, and judgments that clutter your life and are at odds with your spirit. You have a choice to change what isn't working for you or is causing you a conflict.

You know that certain functions like breathing and heartbeat are essential for life, while others, such as sex, passion, and happiness are not. When a conflict ensues, your energy is diverted to the conflict. Eventually something will give. You may lose interest in sex, or live in a state of numbness, while convincing yourself you are happy. When your tribal beliefs conflict with your soul, your vibration drops, your inner light dims, and you open yourself to physical, emotional, and spiritual maladies.

This doesn't mean you have to give up your tribal heritage and throw away everything you own, but simply the items that cause a conflict or that do not raise your vibration or allow you the life you want and deserve. It's like taking a closer look at that rickety old chair you inherited from your great-aunt that's gathering dust in your bedroom—you know, the one you don't even like—and deciding that maybe your life would be less cluttered without it. In fact, that old chair is an eyesore that drains your energy every time you think about it. But because, like the belief *Hard work makes you a better person,* it was passed down to you by someone who loved you, you are supposed to keep it. So you waste your energy trying to force yourself to keep it.

You need to consciously and happily—not forcefully—decide what to keep, what will raise your vibration. The good news is that when you do an inventory, you will also find some excellent tribal beliefs—and only you can be the judge of what is excellent for you. If they raise your vibration, you may want to pass them on to your children.

But if you are keeping things or ideas that don't make you happy because of a tribal belief, you will lower your vibration. If you find yourself playing mental Ping-Pong, there is simply too much debate and your conflict will lead to feeling guilty.

- Each time you feel guilty, it's a great time to explore the belief that has caused it.
- Each time you find yourself struggling in a game of mental Ping-Pong, look to your limiting tribal beliefs.
- When you have to force yourself to do something, or start your day with, "I should," you cease to be authentic and spontaneous. Explore the possibilities of rewriting your belief.

If a tribal belief is not raising your vibration, then at least *consider* letting go of it like that rickety old chair, even though it belonged to your great-aunt and the tribe expects you to hang on to it.

How to Earn Your Free Lunch

Do you apologize for your happiness? When I ask clients if they have a right to be happy, to make money, to heal, most reply yes. Yet, when I point out the ways they try to earn it, apologize for it, and will even struggle for it, they sheepishly laugh with embarrassment. Underneath that sweet and superficial smile, however, is resentment and anger.

The resentment comes from a limiting belief that unconsciously drives you to earn any goodness in your life. The energetic currency you pay with—your time, your sacrifice, your hard work—will deplete your energetic system and result in smoldering frustration and resentment. Eventually that resentment will make it difficult to celebrate someone else's good fortune. The good news is that you are in charge of the level of resentment you carry. I'll not only show you the subtle ways you do this, but how to heal it.

You get resentful when you don't take care of yourself or listen to your spirit. This includes not speaking up for your needs, accepting assignments that would tax your free time or stress you, or allowing someone to step over your boundaries and not saying anything about it. You carry that resentment energy in your second chakra (the spiritual energy center just below your navel). As the second chakra is the seat of resentment and the seat of your chi, harrah, life force, or passion, if you stuff the chakra with resentment there is little room for the birth of passion. If you smother your chi with resentment, you'll feel tired and sluggish. And if you hold enough resentment long enough, you'll lock up and cause problems in the lower abdomen. They include

- Infertility.
- Uterine fibroids, menstrual pain, dysfunctions of the uterus and ovaries.
- Penile performance issues, prostate problems.
- Loss of your sex drive.

If that last one isn't enough to get your attention, how about this: resentful people age faster—especially the face—because of all the negativity they carry. Okay, now I have your attention, so let's look at those subtle ways you pay for your happiness— which builds resentment—and what to do about it.

I once did a Reading for Lila, a young professional woman working in the world of high finance who couldn't figure out why she felt paralyzed asking questions of people and standing up for herself in negotiations in business. She also said she wanted to "love my life" and "to find my purpose." She assured me her problems related back to how her father, an angry and withholding man, had treated her when she was young. True, this man did absolutely affect her, but the real effect was not the trauma. It was the tribal belief she maintained a staunch loyalty to that said *Everything must be earned.* It was straightforward and simple. And ruining her life.

She reported that while she had some considerable talent writing, she found it to be a painful process and didn't like it. I told her the problem was simple; she was not writing about things she felt passionate about. I saw that as soon as she gave herself permission to write about what she knows about, she would have quite a blossoming writing business if she wanted it. However, that pesky limiting belief stood in the way of her writing coming easily. That would mean she hadn't really earned it.

Her self-esteem was low, so I asked her to tell me something she did that she really loved. She said "yoga." What she didn't realize was that her energy plummeted when she talked about yoga—for her, it was not a vibration raiser. I asked her what she liked about it, and she replied, "I like how I feel when it's over—like I've done something important and that feels good." Of course the energy on that was *When I earn something, it's good for me.* There was no joy, happiness, or flow in her description of her yoga experiences. Rather, it was onerous and heavy.

Can you see how her entire life was controlled by this simple tribal belief? She couldn't value who she was—she had to *earn* her self-esteem. She couldn't feel good about a wonderful yoga class unless she *earned* those feelings by struggling with the poses. She couldn't easily negotiate or ask questions in public settings, she had to *earn* the right to speak.

When you struggle with a limiting belief, it's a good sign that you are ready to change it.

There is nothing wrong with earning things. The problem arises when there are no parameters for the experience. Lila's tribal beliefs did not include a description of how much "earning" she had to do. When had she worked hard enough to earn whatever good she was seeking? When did she earn the right to like herself?

The ironic part of the Reading was that Lila was disappointed that her healing didn't require a large effort on her part. In fact, it wasn't hard to fix, and it wouldn't take a long time. Initially, Lila grudgingly rewrote her tribal: *It's reasonable to believe that I can value everything I earn, and a few things that come easily.*

While her rewrite was a start, Lila wanted to find her purpose in life and regain her passion, but still felt she had to earn both. Until she is willing to consider possibilities outside the realm of her limiting beliefs, nothing in her energetic blueprint will change, and she will find the things she wants just beyond her reach—until she earns them.

She recognized that her overpowering need to earn things was in direct conflict with her personal beliefs. She went as far as to say she was mistaken to follow the limiting belief; she was clearly struggling with her thoughts and left determined to begin working on her rewrites.

"Well, the good news is," she said, "I believe we learn best from our mistakes and through trying hard." Lila turned to me sheepishly and laughed. "These tribals really do control what we think and how we act, don't they?"

One of the most effective ways to teach or learn a limiting belief requires no words; your behavior and, most important, your energy, are powerful ways to teach the people around you. When you broadcast the energy of, "I don't deserve to have it easy because I haven't earned it," you are telling people to criticize your ease in life, not to celebrate it—*because you don't value it.*

Taryn came to me because she was feeling chronically tired and a little depressed around the edges. By now, you recognize these as symptoms of someone conflicted and out of synch with his or her spirit. Taryn's overall vibration was as you would expect: it was low, and while I could see that she was a dynamo, her energy was gray and droopy, very much like how she reported she felt.

> *Apologizing for what you want teaches others you don't deserve it.*

Trained as a nurse, she had left hospital work to take on a major position in a corporation. The hours, pay, and conditions were all better than in medicine. The problem was that even a

$100,000-plus salary didn't make up for the loss of meaning in her work. She had courageously decided to return to nursing. I congratulated her; she was obviously listening to her spirit and following its guidance.

But her tiredness remained. And while she was glad to return to nursing, the depression persisted. She couldn't figure out why and wanted it to stop. I took one look at her energy field and the answer was so obvious it nearly knocked me over, even though she was nearly two thousand miles away from me at the time.

I saw a major energy leak because of her relationship with her daughter, Daphne. Taryn was so weakened by her interactions with her daughter that even her self-esteem suffered. All of this was caused by the unspoken energy she broadcast to her daughter: "I'm sorry; I haven't earned the right to be happy." Taryn had divorced eight years ago, and her daughter had never forgiven her, nor had she forgiven herself. Her daughter had been twelve at the time and still blames Taryn for her chronic unhappiness.

Without speaking a word, but by her apology energy, Taryn taught her daughter that she was not a good mother and needed to earn Daphne's forgiveness. Taryn had never gotten over causing Daphne's pain. After all, she believed *A good mother is responsible for her child's happiness.* Her daughter played the part of the injured one quite well, and without words constantly let Taryn know it was all her fault that she was chronically unhappy.

Taryn had since remarried a wonderful man and their relationship was serene and peaceful. I saw no energy leaks there; in fact, it was clear that her current relationship raised her vibration.

Only when her daughter called or came to visit did Taryn's energy change. The transformation was tragic, that of someone begging for forgiveness, filled with remorse and shame but at the same time, she hadn't earned a pardon.

Taryn was filled with apology energy that invited her daughter's criticism. The harder Taryn tried to earn her daughter's forgiveness, the more her plan failed because she kept broadcasting "Forgiveness is earned." She spent tons of money on her daughter, as her personal boundaries faded away. Neither earned her the forgiveness she craved, but it did create a spoiled young woman.

Taryn's Priority Task (the one task that I see in a Reading that will change everything and begin healing) was to forgive herself for her divorce and to ask God for help in this process. I explained that her apology energy was hurting her tremendously and it needed to stop. She was an eager student and, frankly, was ready to feel better, even if that meant having to forgive herself. I asked her to talk honestly with Daphne and explain that she wouldn't apologize anymore for getting a divorce, that Daphne's happiness was Daphne's responsibility, and that she would no longer try to earn her approval. Daphne could like her or not. Further, she had left her corporate job in order to be fulfilled and happy in her work, because she was taking responsibility for her own happiness. (Her daughter had been quite critical of this decision.)

PRIORITY TASK

The one action that will begin your healing.

During the Reading, Taryn's vibration began to pick up as she contemplated letting go of apologizing for her decisions. She felt clear about what she needed to do and felt energized as her plan took shape.

I told her that Daphne would not be thrilled with the new Taryn at first, but that eventually things would work out. Now remember, she had been training her daughter for several years that her mother could be easily manipulated just by her acting a little unhappy. This one cow was being milked heavily, so you can imagine Daphne's surprise when the cow stopped giving milk!

A week later, Taryn reported: "I spoke with my daughter who was critical of my decision to leave a high-paying job for something 'iffy like nursing.' After I assured her that her college funds were secure, I asked if she cares about my happiness. She didn't. She said I had no right to talk about being happy as I ruined her happiness by getting the divorce. Last, I told her I will no longer apologize for getting the divorce and wanting happiness." At this point, Daphne wouldn't talk about it any longer.

This is where Taryn made a sacred choice. She stopped trying to get her daughter to understand. She was pulling back her power, which was something she had not done in her family circle before. Remember, even though she was a strong woman, her apology, her taking responsibility for her daughter's happiness was actually teaching her daughter to be a victim—someone who blames others for her lot in life. And Taryn did this without speaking a word.

Taryn has kept her power and begun to forgive herself; she is more at peace with her daughter's decision to stay angry with her. Taryn feels more energetic, and it's easier for her to speak her truth. She no longer tries to earn what is rightfully hers.

Apology energy will not only drain you, it will teach others that you are open to criticism and judgment. Apology energy will reinforce that you don't deserve to be happy, wealthy, healthy, or successful but that you have to earn your way to make it acceptable to others. It can also teach your children to be victims, something that can cripple them for life if not changed.

To *identify apology energy*, pay attention to how you feel—especially in the stomach area—and how easily you share your information.

- If you notice that your stomach does flip-flops or gets tight, that's a symptom of apology energy.
- When you hesitate and feel uncomfortable telling someone what you are doing, or how much money you made, or how happy you are, it's another symptom of apology energy.
- Telling yourself you need to do or give something to

earn or feel at ease over your good fortune or great decision is another mark of apology energy.

You can *eliminate apology energy* by rewriting limiting beliefs that create conflict because you are happy, successful, or have ease in life.

- Look specifically at your need to earn things.
- Look at your right to be happy when others are not.
- Look at the person to whom you are apologizing—a family member, a coworker, a friend. It will identify the family of beliefs you need to address.

To *identify victim energy*—which is when a person blames others for their bad luck, lack of success, or happiness in life—don't always look for the extreme dramatics of "woe is me, my life is a wreck," or "poor me, I have no choice," or "none of this is my fault." Rather, look to see if it's the fault of the person's boss, God, or someone else—anyone but the person involved.

- Victim energy can be very subtle. When you hear someone say, "It's just my bad luck," or "That's just the way things are," it is an expression of powerlessness. It's a way of saying, "I have no say in my life—alas, poor me."
- When someone routinely becomes angry at events in life and exclaims, "Why me?" they are expressing victim energy.

To *eliminate victim energy,* be honest about the need to blame others for your lot in life because it's easier than making different choices; this honesty will start you on the road to reclaiming your power.

- When you feel the urge to blame someone else, ask yourself whether there was anything you could have done differently in each situation that may have changed the outcome.
- Ask yourself if you neglected to speak up and take care of yourself.
- Ask yourself if you like being angry so you don't have to step up to the plate and grow up and take responsibility for your life.

Be honest, and you will reap a great reward—you will take charge of your life and reclaim your personal power. It will make you more attractive to others and inspire them to do the same.

Please avoid, at all costs, the tragedy of your apology energy colliding with victim energy. Your apology will simply justify a victim's belief that life isn't fair, and the person's powerlessness will intensify your need to apologize.

How Many Martyrs Does It Take to Change a Lightbulb?

Does your struggle and suffering make it easier to accept the goodness in your life—because you have paid for your happiness? For some people, suffering negates the need for an apology. Let me remind you, however, that while pain is a natural part of life, much of your suffering is self-induced. And just like the level of resentment you carry, the amount of suffering you endure is entirely up to you. Change your limiting beliefs about suffering and the subtle ways you cause yourself to suffer, and I guarantee at least 50 percent of your suffering will disappear. (And how many martyrs does it take to change that lightbulb? Absolutely none, because they all just sit in the dark—*by their own choice*—and quietly suffer.)

Three of the four grown children in the Carter family hold to the belief *Suffering is noble,* and they think it will earn them a special place in heaven. Although painful and draining, suffering is viewed as a good thing. The fourth and youngest child, Josh, is different. He is one of those "new age thinkers" and feels at odds with his family's belief system. Josh told me it does not feel like truth to him, and he continually makes choices to diminish his suffering. He knows on a deep level that life can be easy and that suffering is not essential to being a good person. At times, he says, it is difficult to watch his family suffer needlessly. They work all the time, focus on the negative aspects of life, and make personal choices that create more distress. He feels badly for them but no longer attempts to explain his view of life. They just are not interested in changing.

His family sees Josh "skating through life" and is not happy about it. They frequently remark how little he works, how many trips he takes, and how easy his life seems to be. They often remind him that "skating through life" is not normal and that he needs to be prepared for the future because suffering is simply inevitable.

Josh's three siblings live out their lives welcoming suffering and believing it is an essential part of the makeup of a good person. They are passing this belief on to their children. Josh, however, is raising two children of his own, and he's teaching them the new tribal law *Integrity and honesty are noble.* Suffering is not required. In fact, when you suffer, it's easy to forget about the rest of the world. Personal suffering tends to obscure our vision beyond our own pain and to cut us off from community.

How different do you think Josh's children's lives will be from their cousins'? This is an example of two families with different tribal laws, one focusing only on themselves and their suffering, and the other evolving spiritually to focus outside themselves, on their community.

When people rewrite and heal their limiting belief about suffering, they begin to look outward, not inward. There would be more focus in the world on helping others and being of service rather than on one's own wounds or suffering. People's attention would not be on keeping a good reputation (as one who suffers and is therefore noble), but connecting with the person next door who could use some assistance.

It is true there will always be bumps in the road and the inevitable pain. Too often, however, suffering is of your own making thanks to tribal beliefs. It seems there is always one problem or crisis after another. And even the simple problems take a large toll. If you are deeply loyal to the belief *Struggling builds character,* you will not only agonize over the simplest decisions but make mountains out of the smallest of molehills.

You may have also noticed that people who believe *Suffering is noble* reflect unhappiness on the outside, but they are secretly celebrating on the inside. Poor Lancelot from King Arthur's court comes to mind. Did you ever see a more lamentable and sad human being, considered the noblest of knights, who celebrated his suffering because it would take him to heaven?

When you are in the heart of self-made suffering, you can easily get stuck believing things are as they should be. Consider Roxie, raised by Irish immigrant parents who had suffered great discrimination and hardship. For them, survival was truly a struggle. They taught Roxie to expect to struggle as it is a natural part of life. Life just couldn't be easy. Roxie grew up with this knowledge and applied it to everything she did. She expected things to be hard, and she broadcast energy that said, "I have to earn everything I get—nothing in life is free or freely given." As a result, her life emulated her parents', even though her situation was far different and much more comfortable than her ancestors' were. Out of loyalty to her tribe, Roxie didn't enjoy life and made everything harder than it needed to be. When I met her she was carrying several heavy energetic boulders upon her shoulders but felt pleased that she was following in her parents' footsteps. She believed her struggles developed character and made her a better person.

Suffering is often self-made.

Roxie's "character" was displayed on her face: she rarely smiled, and when she did, it was a fleeting half smile that never reached her eyes. She often complained that her life was hard and had no idea why. When I introduced Roxie to her tribal beliefs, she was shocked to find the true reason she struggled but hesitant to change it. She commented that no one in her family had ever *not* struggled, and she feared stepping out of their mold. They wore their struggles as a badge of honor, and if Roxie changed, she would not have been honoring them. But her spirit was tired of the struggle, and she decided to change the beliefs that were so exhausting her.

SOME QUESTIONS TO HELP YOU UNCOVER YOUR TRIBAL BELIEFS

1. Do you believe that life is not meant to be easy?
2. Is it necessary to suffer to learn lessons or grow?

TRIBAL BELIEFS ABOUT STRUGGLING, SUFFERING, AND ADVERSITY

1. Suffering is noble.
2. Suffering is a natural part of life.
3. The more you suffer, the better person you become.
4. Suffering will get you a special place in heaven.
5. No pain, no gain.
6. Depriving yourself of joy shows how much you care about others who are suffering.
7. You can be proud of continually overcoming adversity—even when you cause it for yourself.
8. Only the good suffer.

9. Always suffer in silence.
10. Suffering builds character.
11. Life is filled with pain; it's how you grow.

You might think that Roxie was thrilled to find the cause and solution of her difficult life. The truth is that sometimes, as people grow in their spiritual awareness, they feel worse before they feel better. Specifically, they feel more pressure. They begin to feel the delight of living in a higher vibration and wonder why their families and friends aren't inspired to make the same changes. Then they sometimes start to feel uncomfortable, because they are so happy (but their family and friends aren't), and may sabotage their newfound joy. But now they are acutely aware of when they lose that wonderful, high-vibration feeling. The lows now feel worse because they know what it feels like to live according to their souls. It's like having had back pain for years and suddenly waking up pain-free. It's exciting, but you don't quite trust your good luck. And if the pain returns, it feels even worse because of the contrast.

When you reach this uncomfortable place, it's up to you how long you stay here. Here's what you need to do if you get stuck in that place of suffering and can't get out of it:

- Pray for courage to continue your journey and for comfort as you bravely take a risk and move away from what you thought was true about life.
- Talk to your best friend or partner for support along the way. If that isn't possible, find someone who is neutral and can simply listen.

- Trust that your spirit is guiding you to the right place—it always will.
- Recognize that you have the power to end your suffering instantaneously.
- Celebrate your willingness to consider new possibilities.
- Choose daily to be an inspiration for others.
- Remember that many have walked before you and come through this darkness to find their passion, joy, and health—and you can, too.

I know that initially your families may not always celebrate your newfound freedom, but you always have the choice to belong to many tribes. It's important to find like-minded people on your journey who will inspire you by their success. And know we are here to celebrate your success and that you will one day inspire others—what a wonderful gift you will give others.

8.

Your Most Treasured Beliefs Can Leave You Angry and Resentful

GUILT: A CONFLICT BETWEEN YOUR SOUL

AND YOUR TRIBAL BELIEFS

The reason people come to me is to heal their mind, body, and/or soul. No matter what their problem—whether it's cancer or being unable to trust their divine guidance—I often find a pesky yet quite powerful tribal belief in their way. When I explain that a tribal belief is holding the person back from healing or growing, I'm overjoyed with responses like this:

- "Wow, I had no idea I was doing that. How can I change it?"

- "I can't believe I have that tribal belief, but I do!"
- "Wow, I can see how that has caused many of my problems."

Unfortunately, I get other responses. People will adamantly announce the reason they cannot do what it takes to move forward, heal, or change their life. They are in the bargaining stage of healing a tribal belief; they tell me things like this:

- "Tribal beliefs are fact, law, and true, *and* not to be messed with."
- "It's habit/familiar/easier and simply an automatic response of mine."
- "It's who I am."
- "I don't want to change it."
- "I don't want to take responsibility for the change."
- "I am afraid to hurt others because they might think poorly of me."
- "You should trust authority. They know better than you do."
- "I can't always trust my gut. It has misled me in the past."
- "I must always be in control or chaos will ensue."
- "I do not trust myself without approval or confirmation from others."
- "Keeping my family is more important than me being happy."
- "I need to take care of others before myself."

- "It is not okay to ignore the rules."
- "Things are either right or wrong."
- "I can't change and be healthy and happy if the rest of my family isn't."
- "I feel guilty."

Let's look at the *real* reasons why people won't change some of their tribal beliefs: the guilt because of mistaken loyalty, the fear of being thought of as selfish, and the refusal to forgive themselves.

When Making a Good Change Feels Bad: Guilt

The first common reason for not changing a tribal belief is that you feel guilty. The more guilt you feel, the harder you are trying to hold on to a tribal belief that is in conflict with your spirit. I would like to teach you what guilt actually is and how it can be dealt with. What so many people call guilt is actually not guilt at all. It is important to differentiate between true guilt and the uncomfortable feelings you have when you disappoint the tribe.

There is one true form of guilt. When a person takes a life or betrays another person, the damage to our soul is true guilt. I also call this "sacred guilt" because it is a result of breaking a sacred tribal law: Thou shalt not murder, steal, or be less than human to another being. The damage comes from being so contrary to your true nature. Your mind reels and your conscience is overwhelmed. Healing from sacred guilt is a deeply spiritual issue and requires the accepting of unconditional love, self-forgiveness, and the changing of any tribal belief that interferes with the embracing of full forgiveness and healing.

What most people call guilt is the uncomfortable feeling that results from the battle between what one is supposed to do and what one wants to do. Have you ever watched a friend agonize over a decision? For example, Kara wanted to avoid her sister as much as possible, yet said she felt guilty about it. This feeling of guilt came from trying to follow a tribal belief—*Stay close to family members*—that was not in alignment with her spirit. Her sister was toxic to her. Feeling guilty is the external expression of a conflict within. It's a way to save face with your tribe—it shows that you still care. But it is also a way to avoid facing the truth.

> GUILT
>
> *The conflict between doing what your spirit wants or doing what people expect you to do.*

In your energy system, I can see a big difference between sacred guilt and a conflict that's making you feel uncomfortable. What people usually call guilt occurs when you experience a conflict between your soul and your tribal beliefs. You *know* whether you want to go home for Thanksgiving dinner, continue giving money to that relative who is always in crisis, or spend time talking with a friend who has become negative and complains constantly. The answer is quite clear in your mind. Then your tribal beliefs kick in and start reminding you: *Holidays are for family time, Families help each other during the tough times,* and *A good friend always understands.* Your conflict increases because you refuse to believe that your soul would not want you to do something that you have been taught is essential to being a good and spiritual person.

When you feel torn between your spirit and your tribal beliefs, you feel miserable, filled with conflict, and deafened by mental Ping-Pong. Not infrequently, you may experience physical symptoms like a stomachache or headache—a sign of mind-body-spirit conflict. You see, your spirit is always urging you forward, toward happiness, and into a passionate life. If you were to live honestly and according to your vibration, you would trust your spirit, tell the truth, take care of yourself, and take responsibility for making your life happier.

Guilt leads to powerlessness, and powerlessness is a choice.

Remember I said that as children, we were powerless, but not so as adults. You choose to give away your power—it is not taken away from you, nor are you powerless like a child. The reactions of your tribes can cause you to reevaluate what you know—what your spirit has told you. Their reactions can cause you to doubt your inner voice, only if you choose to give your power away to them.

Maureen felt the pressure of several tribes who said she

should forgo socializing and study hard for months for the bar exam, but her spirit told her she was prepared and she felt confident and ready after three weeks. Her tribe was horrified to learn she took a trip to Mexico to bask in the sun.

Christina lost the lease to her apartment and had two weeks to find a new place, but couldn't take time off from work. Her guidance said not to sweat it—she could look for a new place, but it would make no difference because all would work out easily. Her tribal friends bordered on hysteria at her calm attitude. She found the perfect apartment two days before she had to move out.

The amount of so-called guilt you feel is in proportion to your fear of being disloyal to your family, friends, or colleagues. "Here's a family that loves me and I'm not loving them back," you think. And you aren't—at least not in accordance with their tribal beliefs: you aren't doing what they want you to. If you are very afraid of being kicked out of your tribe, you will work very hard to hold on to a tribal belief even though it is in conflict with your spirit.

GUILT

Trying to force the magnetics where there are none.

Your spirit is naturally more evolved than you are, resulting in a conflict from time to time. The question is, when conflict occurs, how long will it take you to listen and change the tribal belief that is keeping you bound? How long will you let your so-called guilt run your life? I will never forget the time in a workshop when I asked a woman who had the tribal belief *Marriage is forever* how long she had known her marriage was dead. She looked at me intently and said, "Oh, about thirty years." Once your spirit has spoken, have you noticed how the guidance just does not change? For thirty years, this woman had been ignoring the exact same message from her soul and feeling conflicted about going against her tribal beliefs. Her spiritual evolution had come to a standstill. Her choice to ignore her spirit had exacted a toll; she paid the price with unhappiness and illness.

As you evolve spiritually, you will recognize some tribal beliefs that you have outgrown. At this point, you can make a choice to be in alignment with your spirit and mentally accept what your energy system has already embraced. Guilt is the mind trying to hold on to something old and ignoring the voice of your spirit. As long as you do not acknowledge and embrace your spirit, there will be conflict, and thus a drain on your energy. My job is to help you recognize that what you have been experiencing as guilt is really conflict between your spirit and old tribal beliefs you need to change. Draining your energy because of conflicts is something you can stop easily. And it is easier if you know the language of your spirit.

Our spirit expresses itself via the law of magnetics. This is actually the language of your spirit. When you have magnetics for something, you feel drawn to it, energized, passionate, and alive. When you have no magnetics for something—whether it be a relationship, a job, the place you live, a friendship, or a form of exercise, you feel listless, disconnected, and unhappy. Losing magnetics for a friendship can make a phone call to that friend a chore. Losing magnetics for anything can make doing that particular thing boring or just plain difficult.

Sometimes this is called burnout, but it's much more than that. It is your spirit wanting to expand to something else. And it can happen even in areas of your life that you once loved and had great passion for. But once the magnetics are lost, you are out of the flow. Life isn't supposed to be this hard. When we attempt to force magnetics and we go against our spirit because of tribal laws, the result is what people call feeling guilty.

Lisa knew about guilt firsthand. She had relented and allowed her grown son to move back in with her against her better judgment and guidance. When I asked her what she was thinking, she revealed a tribal belief: *A good mother always helps her children.* This is a classic example of a conflict: Lisa's guidance, instincts, and intuition all said, "Don't do this!" But her tribal belief said she'd be a bad mother if she didn't. The thought of not helping her son filled her with guilt. And the son knew this. Being manipulative, he had set himself up in a situation where he was basically homeless and staying in a bad part of town. He called his mom for help. His moving in was the worst thing that happened to Lisa.

Remember, guilt is what kept Lisa up at night. She knew definitively that having her son home would create havoc for her. She knew he was using her and he'd end up causing her a financial fiasco. But Lisa's tribal belief told her she had to help. Only a bad mother would say no to a child in need. Added pressure from her extended family caused Lisa to struggle with her decision for days. No one asked her how she felt or what her gut said. They were there to enforce the law: she must do everything to help her child or risk being labeled (or self-labeled) a bad mother.

After a brief discussion with me, Lisa realized she was staying loyal to an old belief that was lowering her vibration tremendously. Allowing her son to move in had been an immense drain on her energy, finances, and private time. She was trying to heal from cancer and it was hugely important that she use all of her energy for healing. It was also essential that she not drain her energy by feeling guilty (i.e., conflicted) or trying to force magnetics where she had none. Something had to change. Either her desire to heal had to become her primary goal or her tribal belief did.

Faced with a powerful choice that would affect her healing and the rest of her life, Lisa prayed. Should she go with her dynamic, growing self that was aligning with her soul, or stay static, loyal to the tribal belief? She had to make a sacred choice— sacred because it involved her commitment to her healing, her spirit, and herself.

Initially, Lisa chose to remain loyal to her tribe. Shortly after her son moved in, however, she asked him to leave. She could no longer tolerate the tension, the energy drain, or the loss of her vibrancy. Rewriting her tribal belief from *A good mother always helps her children* to *A good mother sets boundaries* resulted in a much happier and healthier Lisa.

Her son was very upset about her decision and immediately blamed his mother for his unhappiness. I encouraged Lisa to look at all her tribal beliefs about motherhood and she immediately found one that created tremendous conflict within her. The belief *Good mothers raise happy children* stunned her. She felt like a failure, and this feeling was driving her to do everything she could think of to make her son happy, even if it ate up what little extra energy she had. Lisa recognized that once again her limiting tribal belief had trapped her in a difficult situation.

I reminded her that everyone has to make choices in life, and these choices directly affect our level of happiness or success. At first, Lisa was shocked by my words. So I shared the joke I had once told to Jerry Lewis, who laughed profoundly. "How many martyrs does it take to change a lightbulb?" Lisa pondered as I continued, "None. They just sit in the dark and suffer."

I watched the lights go on and the great "Aha!" descend upon her. "That's exactly what my son does—he won't get up to help himself, he'll just sit there! I swear he almost seems to enjoy his difficult life, and he seems to resent people who don't struggle. It's like everything is hard for him, nothing ever seems to come easily to him."

This trait in her son tied in to another tribal belief Lisa had: *A good mother can motivate her children to change.* This one kept her tied in to having to offer suggestions to her son, come up with ideas, point out opportunities, and in general be a cheerleader to someone who did not want cheering up. She rewrote that tribal belief to *A good mother shows that change is possible by changing her own life.*

Lisa rewrote several tribal beliefs about motherhood, kept her martyr son out of her house, and is on the road to healing in many ways. She now knows that a good mother takes care of herself, role-models good boundaries, and allows her children to be unhappy if that is their choice. Lisa chose to live vibrationally and honestly. She gently spoke her truth, took care of herself, and took responsibility for making her life happier.

Let me leave you with the perfect antidote to guilt: changing your tribal beliefs does not mean you have to abandon your tribe. It means you make the sacred choice to be a tribal leader, teaching others in your tribe by example to listen to their souls.

So-called Selfishness

The second most popular reason for holding on to a limiting belief is the fear that people will consider you a selfish person. For example, I hear "I don't want to hurt others by being honest—it's selfish." When I point out that this belief can cause simmering resentment and anger, I am given some very high-minded, well-thought-out reasons for not being honest. However, before you think that you are being noble by keeping your Truth to yourself, ask yourself: Is it possible that you are actually afraid of dealing with others' reactions, do you think you won't know what to do or say, or are you more afraid of your reputation being damaged than you actually are of hurting them? Usually I find that at the bottom of "I don't want to hurt so-and-so" is a fear of what the person will think of you when you do tell him or her. The good news is that as you follow your spirit more and more, and your self-esteem builds, you will develop more immunity to feeling bad if others are critical of you or make judgments about you. It is pure freedom to lose your fear of what people think of you.

Always examine your motivation for what you are doing. Are you really trying to make your family happy—or are you afraid they will think less of you? Consider how much of your valuable energy you waste, trying to be all things to all people.

C. S. Lewis is one of my favorite writers. He speaks about selfishness in a way I understand. He explains it this way. Most people believe that thinking of another person's feelings before your own is a selfless thing to do. But when a person holds back his Truth and says it's because he doesn't want to hurt his friend's feelings, he is actually being selfish. The truth is, he doesn't want his friend to be angry with him—he's more concerned with his own feelings than his friend's.

So telling yourself you don't want to hurt others so you can't do what you need to do to heal is just an excuse for not changing. If you want this—and the million other reasons people come up with—to stand in your way, it will. But remember, this kind of thinking keeps you stuck. When you change your tribal beliefs, you become more flexible, more amenable to the flow, more responsive to the whispers of God's voice and the desires of your spirit.

Gary, a successful, financially independent businessperson, was terribly unhappy in his job. His boss often chewed him out, the pressure of his sales quotas was pain-inducing, and he simply did not like the kind of work he was doing. Gary wanted to spend time with emotionally and physically challenged children—by driving their school bus.

The reaction of his tribe was swift and harsh. His coworkers, wife, and extended family all agreed he was crazy. In unison they told him *Everyone knows you do not leave a good job—it provides security.* What a waste of his education, hard work, and success on the corporate ladder it would be for Gary to drive a school bus, they said. Besides, driving a school bus was not a profession. It was no job for a smart and educated man. "It's selfish of you even to consider it," his wife added.

Gary buckled under the weight of the tribe. He became increasingly unhappy and vaguely symptomatic, suffering from back pains, fatigue, and a general apathy. Whenever he started talking about the children and imagined driving their bus, his energy soared. But his tribal beliefs about duty, work, happiness, success, and being a good husband and father had his spirit trapped. Stressed and unhappy, Gary checked into a hospital with an ulcer. Even then, his tribe was relentless.

> *I've never Read anyone who was meant to be unhappy.*

I told Gary he was at a crossroad and it was time to make a sacred choice: listen to your spirit or languish in a self-induced prison. Gary's biggest struggle was with his profound tribal belief about taking care of himself instead of others. It was a struggle he won. After rewriting his beliefs, Gary quit his corporate job and healed his ulcer. And laughs every time he greets one of his children on the bus.

What does it take to be loyal to yourself, loyal to your soul, loyal to the voice of God within you? We are all meant to live at a high vibration. We are hardwired for happiness and love. In all of the Readings I've done, I've never yet seen the blueprint of someone who is meant to be unhappy.

One final note. One of the biggest problems I see with my clients is that they don't know how, forget, or don't take the time to take care of themselves because they are too busy doing for others. Recent research shows that babies as young as eighteen months will try to help if they perceive someone needs help or is in trouble. This means we are also hardwired for altruism. The interesting thing, however, is that a baby will not try to help unless he or she perceives the need to be real.

My point is that it is great to help others in need—including you. But consider taking a moment to identify your motivations for helping so much and to clarify if your help is truly needed in each situation. Are you responding based on your wiring or responding based on a limiting belief? Again, heeding the voice of your spirit can create immense peace within you and guide you to being an authentic person.

SOME QUESTIONS TO HELP YOU UNCOVER YOUR TRIBAL BELIEFS

1. Do you avoid asking for help for little matters?
2. Does asking for help make you a burden?

3. Do you give a lot but get little recognition for it?

4. Do you ever feel resentful about giving too much? (This last question is important because it means you are giving beyond your limits because of a tribal belief—not because you want to give.)

TRIBAL BELIEFS ABOUT SELFISHNESS AND ASKING FOR HELP

1. Taking care of yourself is selfish.
2. Think of others before yourself.
3. Give until it hurts.
4. Being of service requires denying your needs.
5. If you have gifts and talents, hide them—no one likes a boastful person.
6. Worry about what other people think of you.
7. It's selfish to bother people with your problems.
8. Only spiritual or good people receive help.
9. Do not ask for help, it makes you a burden.
10. Don't blow your own horn—boasting is distasteful.
11. Don't bother others with your problems, you will appear weak.
12. No one will take care of you but yourself.
13. Your problems are small, and it's not right to ask for help when there are people worse off than you who really need the help.
14. Asking for help means you're weak.
15. If you ask for help and get it, you owe something.
16. Asking for help means losing your independence.

17. If you struggle through on your own, it builds character.
18. Asking for help is embarrassing. It implies you're a failure.
19. Asking for help means letting go of control.

You Made Your Bed, Now Lie in It

To err is human, to forgive is a choice.

The third reason people have difficulty changing a tribal belief is one of the saddest but most firmly held beliefs I have encountered: *Mistakes, transgressions, or sins are not forgivable.* Can you imagine believing you have to pay penance for the rest of your life for getting pregnant out of wedlock? Can you imagine how this penance would overshadow the joy you might experience with your child? What if you lost the family fortune by making a bad investment and berated yourself so much you had no energy left to rise again? Or got so locked into your shortcomings that you neglected to notice your goodness? Or felt that your mistakes were who you really are?

The worst part about this tribal belief is that because you think you can never be forgiven, you sever your relationship with God or your Higher Power and cut yourself off from receiving divine guidance and recognizing synchronicity at work in your life.

❧ ❧

Diane is strong, independent, successful, and angry. She had one moment of vulnerability that left her alone and pregnant at twenty-five. She vowed never to repeat her mistake and never has. For thirty years, she has lived with this stain upon her breast, like Hester Prynne in *The Scarlet Letter.*

Convinced that God is waiting to smite her, every difficulty Diane faces—and most are of her own making—feels like a punishment from God for making such a dreadful mistake. Compounding the problem is her son, Mike, a brilliant guy who marches to the beat of a different drum. Mike's disdain for ordinary societal rules and his choice to live his life his way have convinced Diane that she is a bad mother. Mike is just one more piece of evidence that she doesn't deserve forgiveness.

The irony is, Diane takes great pleasure and pride in the difficulties she attracts to herself, hoping they will expunge her past. Her belief system is rigid and powerful, and rather black and white: having sex before marriage meant a lifetime of suffering. I asked her how many years of penance would even the score with God, and she said, "All of my years on this earth won't even the score." I asked if she were willing to consider a different reality—maybe a different God, one that is loving and helpful. She said, "Absolutely not!"

How wretched and rigid a life. Diane's self-imposed suffering has eaten away her self-esteem and left her alone. Her pain is ten times greater because she wants to suffer. She needs to prove that she is special, one of the only people on the planet who had premarital sex that God will not forgive.

When we hold on to our sins, we teach our children to hold on to theirs.

I ache for people like Diane. It simply doesn't have to be this hard.

Many people I have worked with suffer from variations of not being able to forgive themselves. They are forever seeking to "pay for" their sins through a variety of means. Often it involves delaying or denying themselves ease or pleasure in their lives, living with low self-esteem, locking themselves into a difficult situation and then not taking action to get out, or just holding on to the distance between them and God. I see the immense waste of energy and how their lives are affected by beliefs that prohibit them from letting go of whatever they did and moving on. Feeling badly about making a mistake is natural, but punishing yourself forever is never appropriate.

I urge you to fully examine your beliefs about mistakes and forgiveness. Most people cannot answer this simple question: "How much penance is appropriate to expunge your mistake?" I have seen countless people who are continually punishing themselves in an infinite variety of ways because of a perceived transgression in their past. Holding yourself to a so-called higher standard (others could be forgiven for this, but not me) does not make you a better person. It only makes you a more miserable person. Stop the berating (it's a choice). Making your life more difficult, delaying your happiness, or sabotaging your good are no way to make penance.

Instead, you might try this three-step method to come to forgiveness:

1. Admit to yourself exactly what you have done. And it may not be what you think. I have worked with women who feel they let their children down because they were ill, angry, depressed, or involved with drugs or alcohol while their kids were growing up. The guilt and remorse they feel is immense, especially if they were the only parent their child had. They think what they did wrong was to be unavailable to their children. The real mistake I usually see in their past is that they neglected to care for themselves, which led to a downward spiral of resentment and anger, which led to depression or alcohol abuse. Note how you did not take care of yourself—did it make you short with your children? Resentful of another's happiness? Did you sleep with someone you shouldn't have? Listen to your spirit and find out the motivation for your actions. The motivation will shed light and lead to the real transgression that needs forgiving.

2. This is simple but crucial: you must understand your mistake and commit to never doing it again. This means you take *spiritual responsibility** for your life and you determine to stop whatever negative behavior or thinking patterns have created your

* Accepting responsibility for your vibration and making choices that raise it.

suffering. This usually involves rewriting some tribal beliefs, and this book will help you do it.

3. Third, you must change every tribal belief you have that says there is no forgiveness for mistakes. You must choose—yes, it is a choice whether you criticize yourself or not. It is a choice if you focus on the worst parts of you, rather than the good. If you are having difficulty, then focus on helping someone in need, rather than wasting your time and effort on chastising yourself. Do something positive. Choose to ask for help—from God, your spiritual adviser, or your friends. Be honest and admit that you are in charge of how you treat yourself, and start treating yourself the way you would a friend.

SOME QUESTIONS TO HELP YOU UNCOVER YOUR TRIBAL BELIEFS

1. Can you forgive someone else for making the same mistake as you, but not be able to forgive yourself?
2. Do you believe that if you forgive yourself too quickly, it means you don't care?

TRIBAL BELIEFS ABOUT MAKING MISTAKES AND FORGIVENESS

1. I have to make amends for my sins the rest of my life.
2. If I repeat a mistake, I am a bad person.
3. There are some mistakes that can never be forgiven.
4. Good people don't forgive themselves too easily.

5. Sinning makes me a bad person, and bad people are not forgivable.

6. Penance lasts a lifetime—it keeps me on the straight and narrow.

7. If I had high moral standards, my mistakes would bother me more.

8. Mistakes require punishment.

9. Suffering is punishment for making mistakes.

10. God is vengeful and unforgiving.

11. God will punish me for my mistakes—it's only fair.

12. You have to earn forgiveness.

13. Once you screw up, you never recover from it.

Earlier I mentioned that forcing yourself to do things you don't want to do—because of feeling guilty or worrying about your reputation—will cause feelings of resentment, frustration, and even anger at the people you care about. Now I'd like to explain those feelings, and if you are willing to be honest and explore your role in creating resentment, I'll show you an easy way to heal it.

Healing Your Resentment

The level of resentment within you is in direct proportion to your level of self-care. Self-care includes

- Being authentic about your feelings, needs, and desires.
- Maintaining strong personal boundaries.

- The level of personal power you claim (the times when you choose *not* to be a powerless victim who blames others for your situation, but rather you speak up and take care of yourself).
- The amount of leisure time you devote to yourself (relaxing, sleeping, meditating, dancing, hiking).
- The amount of discomfort you will endure before speaking up or making a change in your life.
- How much you judge, criticize, or berate yourself.
- How much you let negative people affect you (will you stay in an abusive or negative situation, rather than remove yourself?).
- How willing you are to give your power away and let another's opinion of you (your art, your beliefs, your clothing, your job) damage and lower your self-esteem.
- The level of self-forgiveness you afford yourself.

High resentment levels mean little or no self-care.

Whenever you forget to nurture and care for yourself because it feels selfish, your level of resentment will rise. To heal your resentment toward others:

1. You need to identify how well you take care of yourself. Are you a people-pleaser who forgets to

please him- or herself? Refer to the list above to identify ways to take care of yourself.

2. You must take personal responsibility for your level of self-care—that means not blaming others because you are stuck cleaning the garage while your husband is off playing golf. Why are you not doing what you want to be doing?

3. Focus for one week on self-care and actually nurture yourself. Make yourself a priority for seven days. Do things that raise your vibration. Speak up for your needs. Make choices that make you happy.

4. Remember to look for the subtle ways you forget to honor yourself. If you come last in your life, your level of resentment will be high.

Lori is intelligent, assertive, and doesn't care to marry. Most of her family snicker behind her back and call her a gay bitch or say she's too ugly to marry. They constantly ask, "What's wrong with you? Don't you like men?" In fact, their tribal beliefs defined her long before she was born. Had Lori's siblings stopped long enough to really look at her, they would have found an attractive, funny lady with many friends, a commitment to her community, and a full life. But all they saw was an unmarried woman.

If you apologize for what you want, you won't get it.

Lori wanted desperately to please her family so she compromised her spirit by getting married to an acquaintance whom she clearly didn't love. The loneliness she endured each night in bed was almost too much to bear. She assumed her wifely duties and had sex with a man without any intimacy. She acted the good wife each day, hiding her pain, hoping to find redemption with her family. After a year of being someone she was not, she thought her family would leave her alone. To her horror, now they complained about her lack of children. "It's been over a year," they'd lament. "What are you waiting for? You aren't getting any younger."

Lori was trapped in a nightmare that seemed to hold no option but sacrificing herself further for the tribe. She became frustrated, resentful, and depressed. Her physician tried her on a multitude of antidepressants, but nothing seemed to work. Her final act before consulting me was to contemplate suicide.

I explained to her that the antidepressants would not work until she worked on the predisposing factors for her depression that stemmed from her resentment. There are two reasons why she became resentful—both of which were in her power to change:

1. She didn't speak up for her needs. Lori needed to tell her family to butt out of her life and stop asking when she would get pregnant—and mean it!

2. Lori set wishy-washy boundaries, which energetically tells people to feel free to step over

them. Her desire to be liked, maintain a good reputation, and be a people-pleaser allowed her to give away her power.

Lori felt resentful because she had compromised her boundaries—she had sex with a man when she didn't want to, she stayed in a marriage in which she didn't belong, and she allowed her family to imply she was less than a woman on many occasions.

We worked on rewriting her tribal beliefs and creating secure energetic boundaries. She realized how unfair their relationship was to her husband and amicably they parted. Next she set herself free by moving halfway across the country. In the beginning she found it difficult to stand up to her family, and it was much easier to avoid them. But eventually she rewrote her tribal beliefs about family, parents, and being a woman, and now has a good relationship with them. Whenever she feels resentful, she immediately looks to see the role she played in those feelings and works to fix it.

She took a healing sabbatical from her family and devoted six months to learning to accept herself as she was and to live at a high vibration. She is medication free and happy to boot.

To heal your resentments, it's crucial to look at your personal boundaries. If you are afraid to tell people the truth—because it might hurt them—you will compromise yourself by doing things you don't want to do and eventually will be angry about it. Feeling guilty or selfish because a tribal belief limits you from being authentic will cause you to create very soft boundaries, and when people plow through them, you'll be upset.

Maintaining soft boundaries is another way of not taking care of yourself. If your energy does not back up your words, you have wishy-washy boundaries. For example, when you tell your children to clean their room, but your energy says, "There will be no consequences," it should be no surprise when they don't listen. When you tell your coworker you need to get some work done—to stop coming into your office—and he or she ignores you, there's a reason. It's because your energy says, "I want you to think I'm a nice person, so I'll listen to you even though it cramps my day."

Many people think they are strong because they have powerful jobs or run large companies. But personal boundaries have nothing to do with your exterior—it's all part of your energy broadcast. Here are some examples of weak boundaries that teach people how you will react to them:

- Have you ever watched a parent tell a child to stop misbehaving and the child doesn't listen? That's because the energy behind the "stop" says, "Keep making a scene in this store and I'll bribe you with a toy or candy to be quiet."
- Have you ever wondered why male coworkers tell dirty jokes in front of you—even though you've asked them not to? Consider what your energy is broadcasting.
- Have you ever told a group of friends you don't like

to gossip or listen to sexist jokes, but they continue to tell them?

- And for you healers out there—ever wonder why your clients call you at late hours, or continually try to squeeze in an appointment when there is no space, or try to stay later than their allotted time? Check out your energetic boundaries.

Here are the tips to leading a happier and more authentic life and healing those resentments:

- Reconsider your definition of selfishness.
- Rewrite your beliefs about so-called selfishness. (*It is reasonable to believe that I can give to others and still take care of myself.*)
- Recognize that "feeling guilty" means you are in conflict with your spirit. You are trying to be the person others want you to be. You are not being authentic or in integrity. Feeling forced to do things will leave you resentful.
- Be honest about the strength of your boundaries. You can't blame others for ignoring your boundaries—your energetic intention and broadcast is telling them what is acceptable or not.
- Take responsibility for your feelings. Other people do not take advantage of you and your kindness—you allow it.
- Open a dialogue with your friends and family and announce your intentions to take better care of yourself.

You'll be surprised at the positive support you will receive.

- Be honest about your motivation for giving and doing so much for others. When your motivation is attached to your reputation, and not a clean place of giving, it will warp into resentment.

- When you are aware of an unclean motivation, stop what you are doing and take some time to reconnect with your authentic self.

- When you are so invested in what others think of you, it's because you have an injured third chakra (the spiritual energy center located in the solar plexus and the seat of your self-esteem, courage, and confidence).

Following are some techniques to begin healing your third chakra from my book *Guidance 24/7*. The more self-esteem you have, the more authentic you will be and the less resentful you will become.

Acknowledging your gifts and talents fills you with a sense of self-esteem—so you are not consumed by the need for approval to boost your reputation. It allows you to own your personal power and not give it away to others. When you have good self-esteem—which you develop by making commitments to yourself that you keep, valuing your personal code of honor, owning your gifts and talents, and letting go of false humility—you do not look for attention or validation from others. If you know you are an ethical person and someone calls you unethical, you don't fall apart. Your strength is inside; you know your worth. The winds can blow until the cows come home, and it has no impact.

What's more, when you don't own your talents, such as painting well, being a good listener, being able to stay cool in an emergency, having a good sense of humor, or being a good friend, you are dishonoring God.

Think of it this way. When you fill out a resume, do you neglect to mention your abilities or talents in your field? If you did, wouldn't it dishonor all the people who taught, mentored, or otherwise helped you learn and grow professionally over the years? Besides, what employer would want to hire you? Owning all of your talents—in every field—builds your self-esteem and frees you from being stuck in your pride. You can have true self-esteem instead of the false self-esteem that comes from things like basking in your ability to constantly overcome adversity and tough things out.

Many people believe it is boastful to acknowledge their gifts and talents. Their family has taught them never to blow their own horn. I can't tell you how many clients have this tribal belief. Are you ready for the truth about this one? The false modesty of ignoring or downplaying your gifts and talents is a slap in God's face. You received a gift, yet will not own it.

What's more, if you hide behind false modesty, you'll never acknowledge who you are, you'll never know what you are capable of, and you'll never develop the courage to get out in the world and try something new—start a relationship, go on a safari in Africa, get out of a bad marriage, or trust God when you are told to leave your job.

Here are ten ways to assess and boost your current level of self-esteem. Put your answers in a log entitled "Who I Really Am." Refer to it often. I cannot emphasize enough how important this is to your spiritual evolution.

1. **Find out who you are.** Describe yourself on paper as if you were writing about a friend. Be honest and list at least five wonderful things about yourself.

2. **Determine what qualities you have that you can always count on.** Write down why you would choose yourself as a partner on a two-week expedition across the Canadian Rockies. Do the same thing with a six-week assignment to work closely together in your profession. If you find a good reason to dread that six-week assignment with yourself, consider changing that behavior. You can always make the choice to do so.

3. **Identify and own the positive things your friends, coworkers, and/or family say about you.** If nothing comes to mind, ask them why they like you. For example, I heard this comment over and over in the ER: "Christel, I love working with you because you know your stuff, and no matter what happens—even if we get a busload of hemophiliacs who've been hit by a train and there's no clotting factor 8 in the hospital—you remain totally calm and get the job done. We feel safe working under you."

4. **Examine how you speak about yourself to others.** Do you say, "I can play the piano"? Or do you say, "I play the piano well," or "I play with great feeling"? Notice when you downplay your abilities, and see if a tribal belief may be responsible. If so, *rewrite it!*

5. **Notice how you respond to compliments.** Do you receive them with embarrassment? Do you protest or brush the comment aside? Next time, button your lip, make eye contact, take in the compliment, and say thank you. Then write the compliment down in your log.

6. **Be aware of how you respond to genuinely constructive feedback.** Do you feel deflated? Do you get defensive or start explaining or rationalizing your behavior? Do you give your power away to the other person? Or do you listen, choose to consider what's been said, and eventually get back to that person for clarification, agreement, or disagreement? Next time, take a breath while you listen, and make an agreement with yourself to look honestly at the person's feedback. Write about the experience in your log.

7. **Pat yourself on the back for your achievements.** Do you notice the good you do or only the mistakes and failures? Think of two things you did during the day that were good for you, for someone else, or for the overall vibration of the planet. Put

them in your log. If nothing comes to you, then simply say a prayer for yourself and one other person.

8. **Respect who you are.** If you don't, why? What could you do differently so you would respect yourself? Pick one part of you that you would like to change, then focus on it for two weeks. Use your log. Make the commitment, and you'll be amazed at the result.

9. **Think about the commitments you make to yourself and others.** Do you keep them? If not, figure out why you commit to things you don't really want to do in the first place, and learn to say no. When you commit only to things you really, really want to do, you will be very pleased at your success rate.

10. **End your day with gratitude for your gifts and talents, your health, and the beauty of a single flower.** Before falling asleep, remember three wondrous things in your day, and tell God how grateful you are for them.

Remember, when you downplay who you are, it does not serve anyone's highest good. Rewrite those tribal beliefs, fill yourself to the brim with self-esteem, and enjoy your life! How would you rather your gravestone read: "Here lies Mark, a hard worker who struggled to overcome adversity"; "Here lies Arlene and she was right"; or "Here lies Tess, a wondrously compassionate woman who could admit when she was wrong and played a mean piano"?

And if that doesn't compel you to start changing, let me remind you of one of my favorite sayings: "Well-behaved people rarely make history." You want to do something with this life— live out your purpose. Don't waste your precious energy on things that don't matter.

9.

What Is Truth for You?

As a Medical Intuitive I have seen and heard many things—it takes quite a lot to shock me. Clairvoyant since age eight, I Read souls for a living, and I know a person's deepest secrets. During an intuitive Reading, I see a running "video" of your childhood at lightning speed. This video reveals the traumas you have endured, your personal beliefs about yourself, your level of self-esteem, your tribal beliefs, and more. It doesn't matter how much personal reflection a person has done, after a Reading or workshop I hear a similar theme repeatedly: "Christel, you know things about me that I never knew—yet as I listen to you, they feel so familiar, as though I knew them at one time and forgot them."

What these people are describing is Truth—which is quite different from something being true. Truth is the language of the soul or spirit, and it is communicated in many forms:

- The spoken word—as when a friend says the most simple yet profound thing to you, like "You know, if you have such a hard time dealing with your step-father and it always leaves you drained, don't deal with him."
- A feeling, intuition, inspiration, realization, sense of knowing, or an "Aha!" moment—as when the twenty-four-year-old Michelangelo envisioned a raw lump of marble and felt the Pieta inside it.
- Synchronicity—as when a coincidence, a sign, a chance encounter, or an unexpected experience confirms what you already know.
- Guidance from God or your Higher Power—as when you sincerely utter a simple prayer, like "Please help me," and, listening, you get an answer.

You are unable to ignore Truth when it first comes to you because it causes that cha-ching effect that reverberates and resonates through every cell in your body. You can actually feel it. The effect of experiencing Truth is so profound a moment, it will:

- Shake you up by confirming what you already knew but were afraid to know.
- Liberate you from the world of illusion.
- Leave you with a sense of profound gratefulness.
- Reconnect you with your soul.
- Tell you your next step in your spiritual journey.

Truth is something you came into this world knowing but have forgotten because you stopped listening to your spirit and started acting the way you were taught according to your tribe's beliefs. This is the beginning of conflict as the voice of your spirit gets silenced and you struggle to do the right thing. Eventually, some people can't hear their spirit anymore and operate with only the mind-body connection. But the spirit is relentless. It is the essence of who we are, and it leads us toward happiness even when we ignore or forget about it.

Getting Unstuck

Remember I said that you can't just rewrite a toxic tribal belief by stating the reverse? There are two reasons for that. First, the reverse might not be the right belief for you. Aligning with your spirit requires you to be aware of your vibrational response to a particular tribal belief. Second, often the best way to start changing a tribal belief is to give yourself some wiggle room. You don't have to turn black into white all at once. Try a few shades of gray. I used this technique with the man who told me, *Only stupid people pray to God for help. Smart people help themselves.* I asked him, "Is it reasonable to consider asking for help once in a while?" Using the word *reasonable* enabled him to open the door on a new belief.

This is what I call giving people some "wiggle room." I show them that they don't have to go to extremes when they rewrite their tribal beliefs. And once they can say yes to a new belief, no matter how many qualifiers it has (It *might* be *reasonable* to think that *sometimes* it's *not a bad idea* to ask for help), they will eventually go further with it. They just need to give themselves a little wiggle room, and they're off and running!

> *Ignoring the urgings of your spirit takes more effort than making changes in your life.*

Here are some great examples of new tribal beliefs that are in the wiggle room stage of being rewritten. Read them aloud and see if they raise your vibration. If so, consider rewriting them in your own words, words that go "Cha-ching!" for you.

- It's reasonable to believe that I can enjoy *some* happy moments.
- It's reasonable to believe that *sometimes* the rug gets pulled out from under us—things do happen unexpectedly, but not always.
- It's reasonable to believe that if something does happen, I can handle it, as evidenced by the times I've done it in the past.

- It's reasonable to believe that parts of the world are not safe, but I have a choice about where I go or not.

- It's reasonable to believe that when *some* people say, "I love you," they actually mean it.

- It's reasonable to believe that I can count on *some* people.

- It's reasonable to believe that my fear does not have to *always* overwhelm me.

- It's reasonable to believe that I can choose to take *better* care of myself now than in the past.

- It's reasonable to believe that taking care of myself makes it easier for me to take care of others.

- It's reasonable to believe that asking for help *sometimes* is okay.

- It's reasonable to believe that honoring myself is a way of thanking God for my life.

- It's reasonable to believe that taking care of myself teaches my children to do the same.

- It's reasonable to believe that owning my gifts and talents allows me to shine brighter—and gives permission for others to do the same.

- It's reasonable to believe that owning my gifts and talents allows God to work through me more *fully*.

- It's reasonable to believe that downplaying who I am doesn't serve anyone.

- It's reasonable to believe that I can continue to live and enjoy life after a loved one has died.

- It is reasonable to believe that *not all* relationships re-

quire a lot of work and that some are actually easy
and fun.

- It's reasonable to believe that berating isn't justified
  just because it comes from someone I'm related to.
- It's reasonable to believe that some people simply
  have a low vibration (gossips, criticizers, and cynics)
  and are not healthy for me, even if they are blood
  relatives or I've known them for a long time.
- It's reasonable to feel pain when someone dies, but it
  doesn't have to be 24/7 to prove I cared.
- It's reasonable to ask God to lift my pain.

And the most important one of all:

- It's reasonable to believe that I can choose to let go of
  my old beliefs any time I want to.

Becoming unstuck also requires honesty. You may not always like what you learn about yourself, but having the knowledge is the first step toward healing yourself and even others.
It's not just for the benefit of your soul but for the benefit of
others'. Each of us has a profound ripple effect on those
around us. When you are happy, you raise the vibration around
you. When you are resentful, you can drag down an entire party.
How do you want to influence those around you?

Your vibration is energetically broadcast to those around
you—and to your children. If you don't want to get unstuck for
yourself, do it for them.

Consider the many fathers and mothers who did not plan

on nor necessarily want to become parents, but who did so because of deeply ingrained tribal beliefs. The saddest part is that on some level, the children always know they're considered an inconvenience and their very presence is resented. Remember, you always communicate energetically, and with training most people can Read energy with varying degrees of sensitivity. Children, on the other hand, need no training. They Read energy very well. Imagine the fear and confusion these children experience when they recognize that while Mom and Dad seem happy and loving on the outside, their energy says otherwise. These children learn that they are not deeply and completely valued. Growing up with this knowledge severely inhibits their self-esteem, courage, and confidence. It can cause them to seek out love and acceptance in untoward places and with the wrong people.

Warren is an amazing young man. At fourteen, he has learned some harsh truths: First, his mother never wanted to be a mother and quit being one when he was four. His father is gay but held tribal beliefs that he should marry and have children. Naturally, the parents' divorce caused a safety issue for Warren. He is terrified in stores if he cannot actually see his father. He lies awake at night, wondering when his dad will quit being his dad.

Warren learned to cope with his fear and pain by dissociating from his body. He is a teenager who feels nothing. He keeps himself wrapped so tightly, he rarely laughs, smiles, or even feels sad. All he knows is fear. Yet, Warren's parents think he is doing well. In fact, they comment how easily he dealt with their divorce.

When I Read Warren's energetic blueprint, I saw a young

boy losing the battle of containing his pain. I saw a bright and sensitive lad who had shut down his heart and barely resided in his body. He worries constantly about doing everything right so his parents will stop being angry. He parrots their opinions and rarely thinks for himself. This sweet child is locked in prison— and getting thinner each day. Eventually, it may become hard to see his energetic blueprint, as he simply fades away.

When an aunt brought laughter, ease, and fun into Warren's life, his parents rebuffed her. They taught him that life is not about having fun; it is about being serious, responsible, and obedient to tribal law.

I worry about children like this. For their sakes, I ask you to examine your tribal beliefs and consider being authentic in order to diminish their confusion and fear. If you hate being a parent, hire someone else to nurture and guide your child and take time for yourself. Find out what makes you happy and make the necessary changes to raise your vibration. Own your choices in the past and the present. Make the choice today to live at a high vibration and share it with the world.

> *You cannot know your purpose in life when you are avoiding what you know, but don't want to know.*

Getting unstuck in life can be easy if you are willing to *find out what you know that you don't want to know.* When you need to leave a relationship, you know well in advance of your departure. You know when your job drains you and it's time to leave—you just don't want to know it because it will require change. You think it's easier to avoid these truths and stay with the status quo, but it's not. Avoiding your Truth (the voice of your spirit) takes a lot of time and energy. Eventually it will lead to deadened feelings as it becomes too uncomfortable to live out of integrity.

I know that ending relationships, changing jobs, and moving to a different state can be hard and painful. But the longer you avoid what you already know, the harder it becomes to wake up each morning with joy, passion, and enthusiasm for the day. Eventually you will become tired, apathetic, and bored with your life, because you cannot find your purpose when you are avoiding what you know. Ignoring your spirit takes more effort than making some changes in your life. Remember that your spirit is tenaciously fighting for your highest good, even when the information seems to fly in the face of all logic or feels too difficult to face.

I did a Reading for a seven-year-old girl and her mother. Chris was bright, beautiful, and wise beyond her years and captured everyone's attention. She was a pure delight but had developed mysterious ailments that confused and bewildered her mother and her community of healers. No one could determine a diagnosis, and little Chris endured multiple time-consuming and uncomfortable treatments without any relief from her symptoms.

If you feel stuck in life, be still and listen to your needs.

One look at this child showed me that her spirit was in trouble. Normally when I look at a person's energy, I see color, texture, and light. This was not so with Chris. She looked like she was wrapped in a transparent gray garbage bag that was ripped, shredded, and leaking. The rest of the Reading confirmed what I saw.

Chris knew her mother did not want to be a mother and secretly resented Chris. This beautiful child lived in abject fear that her mother would leave her one day. Her sense of safety was constantly compromised, and her immune system could not recover from the repeated blows of her ongoing anxiety. Chris needed immediate help.

On the surface, her single mother, Janice, looked like the most devoted, concerned, and involved mother on the planet. She had gone to great lengths to become pregnant and have a natural and healthy childbirth. She fed her child organic and healthy foods, encouraged Chris to get involved in physical activities, was involved in her school programs, and even nurtured her musical talents. Unfortunately, how Janice appeared on the outside did not match how she felt on the inside.

Shrouded in the energy of dark, heavy resentment and anger, Janice wanted nothing more than to be free from her burden. She blamed her unhappiness and depression on her child and energetically broadcast this daily. Chris felt every iota of this energetic broadcast and had decided that her mom would be better off if Chris were dead. Thus her mysterious illness.

Janice, like so many women, became a mother due to her tribal beliefs. She felt she *had* to have a child or else she wasn't a true woman and there was something wrong with her. *Real women want children* was the tribal belief she had inherited. Unfortunately, this message was in direct conflict with her energetic blueprint.

Gifted and creative, Janice had the soul of a wanderer. It wanted her to be free from commitments and travel extensively. She needed a lot of alone time. Energetically, Janice abhorred routine; she found it trapping and confining. When I explained this to her, she spent quite a bit of time fighting me, protesting my findings, and reiterating the immense energy she put into making her daughter's life happy and fulfilling. It was only after Janice realized I had seen who she really was, and she admitted the energetic blueprint that I described was the life she longed for, that she sighed, "Yes, I know. It's all true."

Now, one's Truth may not be pleasant, but it is profoundly healing. Once Janice acknowledged what her spirit wanted, we had something to work with. To my delight, she didn't try to hide her shame or waste time beating herself up for who she was. Rather, she opened an important door. She became willing to change, willing to make amends, and willing to take responsibility for her choices.

I talked to her about honestly connecting with Chris and telling her daughter the truth (even though Chris already knew it). I asked Janice to be present with her daughter and own the fact that she blamed Chris for all her own unrealized dreams. Janice needed to speak from her heart, not out of resentment.

Healing her resentment required honesty. Janice had become a mother not because she wanted to, but because of an inherited belief that *Something is wrong with a woman who doesn't want children.* Janice's desire to keep her reputation as a normal woman and a good woman led her to get pregnant, even though her spirit tried to tell her not to. (It was no accident that Janice had difficulty conceiving or that she had to use multiple sperm donors.)

For seven long years, Janice had harbored her not-so-secret regrets over her decision. Now that she was being truthful, it was time to heal her wounds and those she had inflicted on Chris. She and I discussed relaxing some of her overzealous parenting attitudes, like requiring a seven-year-old to be a strict organic vegetarian and talented musician. Next I suggested that she back off trying to be the perfect parent and stop being a mega PTA mom involved in activities that didn't lift her spirits but left her angry and drained. Then I brought mother and daughter together for a painful but honest talk.

I will never forget the moment when Chris realized that none of her mother's anger was her fault. It was like seeing an abandoned dog finally find a loving home and bask in the healing love. The look of surrender, relief, and joy on Chris's face made us cry. For the first time, Janice saw what a beautiful child her daughter is.

Fortunately, I found in this situation what I so often find: Miraculous solutions are available in a person's life *once that point of honesty has been reached—when you look at what you know but don't want to know.* Janice lived in a town full of people who were dying to be involved in this little girl's life. They knew that Janice wasn't happy being a mom. She agreed to take a major break from parenting and let others care for her child after school, take her on outings, and invite her into their families. The result? A happy village raising a very happy child.

This was a powerful situation where a tribal belief caused the illness of an innocent child—sadly, not an uncommon situation. Fortunately, this mother was willing to place the health of her child before her own need to see herself in a certain light. Both mother and child became happier. Chris relaxed and this brought her immune system back online so it could protect her, as it should have all along.

Janice finally accepted that *Not all women are meant to be mothers* and this didn't make her a bad person. She also realized that taking care of her needs made her happier, less resentful, and able to connect better with Chris. Janice resolved her conflict by looking at her inherited beliefs and making a sacred choice. She realized it was okay that she had not wanted to become a parent. Dissolving this conflict left her with more energy for creativity, which allowed her to find parenting solutions that brought her inner peace, helped her daughter feel safe, and ultimately restored her child's health.

> *Choosing to live at a high vibration will help our planet reach the tipping point toward positivity.*

It's important to remember that we are all connected on an energetic level. Just as one negative person can bring down the vibration and mood of a group, one happy, authentic, and lively person can impact an entire community. When you choose to rewrite your limiting beliefs, you are

- Healing yourself of your dishonesty and unhappiness.
- Healing those around you with your newfound high vibration.
- Inspiring others with your courage to look beyond what you thought was a fact.
- Teaching integrity to your children.

You are adding your high vibration to this planet to help reach the tipping point toward positivity.

Can I Open My Eyes Yet?

One of the most common if not rote responses I hear from people as they uncover their Truth and consider making changes in their life is, "I'm scared," or "It's not safe."

Fear can be a great motivator—as in giving you the strength to open a heavy door during a fire, or in paralyzing you with inaction and making you feel stuck. Your overall blueprint—including your traumas, upbringing, and archetypal makeup—determines your level of fear. Unfortunately, fear takes a toll on the body by weakening the immune system. When you experience pronounced fear in life, rewrite those limiting beliefs first, and then practice the technique that follows to retrain your body to relax and think clearly.

Laura is a kind and compassionate woman with a wonderful career. On the outside she looks like she has it all, but she has a dirty secret. Each morning she has to bully herself to get dressed and face the day. Once in the office she dissociates from her fear and becomes an awesome real estate agent—but only if she can keep her feelings at bay. When she was recently given an outstanding service award, she silently fretted through the dinner, thinking her boss didn't really like her and this was a soft prelude to being fired.

Each time Laura relaxed, became more human, and felt her feelings, she would literally begin to tremble like a small bunny. During her Reading I saw that her mother had narcissistic tendencies and never allowed Laura to feel safely ensconced in their relationship. There was always an unspoken energetic threat to give Laura away if she didn't behave. This threat was the unspoken subtext of a favorite saying of Laura's mom, which was generally uttered with a cool look and narrowed eyes whenever Laura left her toys on the floor: "There are no sure bets in this world."

Laura came away from this upbringing with the "knowledge" that *Nothing lasts forever, Don't get too comfortable because the rug can be pulled out at any time,* and—naturally—*There are no sure bets in this world.* A powerful tribal belief like this can cause serious consequences to your health. In Laura's case, her immune system was compromised; she constantly caught colds and felt run down. She was also too scared to take any fun risks in her life and was immaculate in her housekeeping, secretly afraid that her husband would get rid of her if she didn't keep the house nice. Her self-esteem was quite low even though she was a firecracker at work. After all, if she could be given away (or traded, fired, or left) in an instant because she left her toys on the floor, she wasn't worth very much. No matter what Laura accomplished on the job or at home, she never felt secure.

She focused on retraining her body to relax and was ready to look at her limiting beliefs. Simply rewriting three of her beliefs had a huge effect on her.

- While it's true that nothing lasts forever, I can choose to be fully present and enjoy the good times fully, and not live in fear of the future.
- I can choose to be present in this moment and not worry.
- I am the matriarch of my own tribe and I can retreat to a safe haven each day that I choose.

Today you would find Laura a vibrant, outgoing, and relaxed woman, full of energy. Her immune system is healthy and she describes herself as "a woman lucky enough to begin life at forty-three"!

As Laura learned to feel safe, her immune system got the rest it needed. Not feeling safe wears down the immune system. Remember, our safety first comes from feeling a part of a tribe, a group who will protect each other against the elements. In this day and age, the "elements" might be a sudden need for a babysitter, care during an illness, or temporary housing during a period of financial insecurity. I have done Readings on many people who suffered great blows to their sense of safety in childhood. When a parent is absent due to depression, self-centeredness, addiction, a lack of spiritual connection, or their own fears, a child learns to live without the reassurance and calm that is so important in learning to handle their own fears. A critical or cold parent can create the same fear in a child. Likewise, the absence of a parent through illness, death, divorce, or long separations, such as can occur during military service, can also induce fear in a child. Of course, abuse, whether emotional, sexual, or physical, very often creates profound experiences of fear.

While not everyone who experiences these kinds of childhood traumas develops negative tribal beliefs regarding safety, most do. In my work, I have found that when people live by these unconscious tribal beliefs, the trauma continues long after it has chronologically ceased.

I see a black hole or emptiness in their primary energy center, which is at the base of the spine. I see through a person's exterior—which sometimes looks quite confident—and into their energetic blueprint, which is who they really are. What I see is a fight to feel safe on a daily basis. The person may describe it as always feeling on edge, not trusting the good things that happen in their lives because they are always waiting for the other shoe to drop, for ease or happiness to be taken away from them. Sometimes they describe it as a need to always be prepared because *You never know what's going to happen.* Others describe their fear of "never doing anything right, like I'm always going to be criticized." Always I see an underlying anxiety, the degree of which ranges from a mild state of chronic fight-or-flight to an overt anxiety disorder, and, at its most severe, to an energetic condition I have termed the "scared bunny syndrome." I call it this because it is what clients like this look like to me: startled bunnies, too scared to move and trembling with fear.

This chronic underlying fear keeps the body in a heightened state of awareness. Never fully relaxed, the body is literally in a low level of fight-or-flight. Always on alert, the body pumps out excess cortisol (the body's stress hormone, now known to be responsible for excess belly fat) and adrenaline, the body's own version of speed. It is exactly like revving the engine of your car all the time.

Because the immune system is in a constant state of readiness, it has no time to rejuvenate and thus is more vulnerable. As you know, our immune system is our first line of defense against disease of all kinds. When the immune system attacks itself, thinking it is defending against an enemy, an autoimmune illness is the result. Which organ or tissue is attacked determines the illness, one that my client either has the energetic predisposition for or has already been diagnosed with. Either way, the origin is always the same: a profound lack of safety originating in trauma, loss, or the unspoken fears of adults while the client was growing up. The lack of safety is then kept alive through tribal beliefs.

Feeling such a lack of safety actually wears out the body. This constant drain on the immune system can mean that a person frequently catches colds, has skin problems of all kinds, or feels run down. For some of my clients with a strong constitution, the symptoms of an autoimmune disease are the first warning sign that a breakdown of their immune system has occurred.

Psychologically I see other effects of these tribal beliefs. Many people have a fear of abandonment, but they may not be clear about the beliefs that cause and continue this fear to be active in their lives. When people do not feel inherently safe in life, they often do not feel safe being in their body. Always afraid, they find it easier to mentally drift, to daydream, to not be fully present. Energetically, they literally are abandoning themselves, pulling their energy out and away from their body. This leaves them open to psychic attacks and abuse from others because they are not home. They have an energetic open door where they should have healthy boundaries.

It is not possible to feel safe when you have left your body. When you are not fully aware of what you feel, not completely aware of your environment, and not picking up energetic signals from others, you are leaving yourself open to all sorts of things that are not good for you. Furthermore, when you abandon yourself like that, you are sending out an energetic broadcast that tells others it is quite all right for them to abandon you, too. You are giving them permission to not listen to your feelings, not be present with you, not pay attention to you, and not take you seriously. Thus, you attract people who also have abandonment issues, and you never have real, connected, and authentic relationships. Since true intimacy is a beautiful way to feel safe, you are misusing the energy that is meant to help you feel secure. For you, intimacy only adds to your growing fear.

Energetically, it is impossible to move through negative emotions when you are not in your body. So a backlog of feelings develops. Fear, anxiety, and grief get stacked up. This dam of feelings starts to feel very frightening to deal with. Now you have a paradox: not being in your body, which was supposed to make you feel safer, causes you to feel increasingly unsafe. When people do not feel safe being in their body, they are not fully present. That means they don't really feel their emotions, even though they may appear very emotional. There is a huge difference energetically when individuals feel their feelings *mentally* versus feeling them in their body. A person who is out of their body and in their head does not feel emotionally safe to be around to someone who is in his or her body. The person senses the absence, the vacancy, and the vague unease of being with someone who isn't really there. It is distressing and uncomfortable, like being at a cocktail party with only idle chitchat. After a while, you just want to get away and experience something more real.

This is why, when people have tribal beliefs that make them feel unsafe, they actually induce a feeling of abandonment in others. In other words, it's contagious, and the only way to be immune from it is to have yourself well grounded in your own sense of safety. So you can see why, when parents feel unsafe and are not fully present, without saying a word they can communicate this fear to their children and teach them that constant fear is an appropriate way to feel.

Continual fear weakens the immune system.

Perhaps the biggest problem with those who do not feel completely safe is that they spend immense amounts of time playing mental Ping-Pong. They are often in conflict, so making decisions is difficult. They play mental games of trying to justify, analyze, or figure out each decision because they do not know what they really feel about a situation. And when they do not connect with their feelings, they do not connect with their intuition and guidance. To me, a person without guidance is like a boat without a rudder. Without a clear connection to the divine, one is left with the yammering of the mind, and that, my friends, is a conversation without end. It is no surprise that many people with safety issues complain of fuzzy thinking or brain fog.

Each decision they must make forces them to choose between their tribal beliefs and the yearning of their soul, which is trying so hard to be heard. Unless a person has reached the point of completely turning away from his or her spirit, it still tries to be heard. But many, many times, our soul, our spirit, our guidance leads us in a direction completely opposite from our tribal beliefs. When people are not wholly connected with their soul, their tribal beliefs speak loudest. Almost always, it will be take the form of a "should." And when a person believes that danger lurks around every corner and the rug is always going to get pulled out, it makes going against another tribal belief very difficult.

Let me give you an example. I did a Reading for a woman who had made a very nice life for herself. Becky had a retail shop in a small town, a circle of friends, and a beautiful cottage she had fixed up that included a prolific garden. Her life seemed idyllic. Yet she came to see me because of a profound yearning she couldn't quite identify. She wanted more—she felt stuck.

Her wonderful life and her spiritual searching had left her thirst unquenched.

I saw clearly that the yearning she was feeling was for a fulfillment of her connection to God or a Higher Power. I saw her leaving her life in the northern United States and going to Arizona where she would study herbal medicine from one of the Indian tribes there. I saw her growing herbs, studying herbal medicine, and being profoundly happy. As I shared this vision with her, she grew more and more animated. "I have always thought in the back of my mind about going to live in a drier climate, and I have always felt called to New Mexico and Arizona.

"But I'm scared. I can't just leave my life here," Becky explained. When I asked her why not, she said, "You just don't pick up and leave when you have a good life somewhere." It was not a matter of financial limitation, the sadness of leaving friends (energetically she was not bonded to her friends, who were actually just acquaintances), or any logistical concern. For her it was strictly a tribal belief that *You don't make sudden changes in life.* Becky also had a profound tribal belief that *Big changes are scary and fraught with danger.*

When I explained to her that the only thing standing in her way was her fear based on her tribal beliefs, Becky was willing to practice a technique to overcome her fears, and began to change quite quickly. She quietly said to me, "I have always wanted to explore the Southwest. It calls to me. I truly do want to live there."

I helped Becky change her tribal beliefs and her vibration began to rise considerably. "I can do this!" she told me. The excitement in her voice was nearly palpable.

I see many clients who have a sense of something they want to do but the fear based on their tribal beliefs is getting in the way. Several tribal beliefs come into play here:

- You shouldn't make big changes after a certain age.
- You have to get more experience first before making a big change.
- Change is scary and overwhelming.
- Big decisions are hard to make.
- You can't recover easily from mistakes.

Very often, they can't tell me what exactly they are afraid of, but get caught in the throes of this nebulous but paralyzing fear, because *change is scary and overwhelming.* Let's find out why you feel unsafe following the guidance of your spirit. Let's find out exactly what you are afraid of.

A Powerful Technique to Triumph over Your Fear

Your spirit has whispered to you that you need to make a change, and you cannot ignore it any longer. Suddenly vague and not so vague fears arise. You fear the disapproval of your community or coworkers; you fear disappointing your parents or friends; and perhaps you fear something is wrong with you and your choice to change. Do any of these decisions speak to you?

- You want to leave a financially rewarding job because you aren't happy with your work.
- You want to change careers—even though you are successful, or spent so much money and time for college and training.
- You need to end a marriage to a nice person.
- You are afraid to think outside the tribe and change a tribal belief.
- You want to change your religious affiliation.
- You've realized your heart's desire—to get on a Harley-Davidson motorcycle and tour the country, but you are afraid of the reactions of your family and friends.
- You want to live an openly gay life.
- You want to take a sabbatical, even though you will lose your position on the corporate ladder.
- You are at the point that you have to face what you already know to be true (and wish were not true), because it has affected your health.
- You need to end a friendship because it is so draining.

The first thing you need to do is to be candid. Are you truly afraid, or are you avoiding a messy situation because you don't want to deal with anything unpleasant? If it is your fear, you have to take a very honest step and be willing to explore the real cause of your fear. Whether you work through it is entirely up to you, but I'll show you a wonderful technique to get you out of your paralysis.

1. Close your eyes, sit quietly, set an intention, or say a prayer for healing. Ask to be shown the information you are seeking. Clear your mind by slowly breathing in and out several times, paying close attention to the sound of your breath, and the rhythm of your breathing.

2. Imagine a beautiful pond set in the woods in autumn. The wind is blowing and the sun is glistening on the colorful leaves. Create the scene based on your vision of beauty, but you must be able to see the periphery of the pond.

3. Envision the wind blowing across the surface of the pond causing waves and ripples. Notice the strength of the wind and the size and speed of the waves and ripples.

4. Focus on slowing the wind and calming the surface of the pond. This may take several minutes.

5. When your pond is still and glasslike on the surface, you are ready to begin. Think about your relationship or job—whatever change is troubling you—and pay attention to the surface of your pond. If the surface becomes turbulent, consciously smooth it out. Continue the process until you can think about what frightens you and the pond surface is relatively still.

6. Ask yourself what frightens you about the change? You may get answers like "I'm afraid to be alone" or "I don't want to hurt anyone." Ignore these

answers because they are on the surface of the pond and not your Truth.

7. Look below the surface of the pond and ask for a more honest answer to your question: What truly frightens you? Listen for the answer.

8. Don't judge or condemn what you hear—it will only distract you. Stay focused on the answer.

9. Ask yourself: Am I afraid for my reputation—that people will think I am selfish, crazy, or a loser?

10. Imagine the worst thing people could say about you if you make this change in your life. Why is it so bad?

11. Identify your judgment or criticism of your action. This will shed light on your limiting belief.

12. Make a small and incremental change to your limiting belief. Begin a rewrite with *It is reasonable to believe . . .*

13. Look below the surface, and watch yourself (like you are watching a movie) move forward with your decision. See yourself speaking to your mate, your boss, or your family. Watch the scene from above the pond—do not immerse yourself in the water.

14. Notice everything in the scene below. Watch for facial expressions and reactions, listen for comments, but especially watch yourself for apology energy as you announce your decision. Say a prayer of gratitude for this information and slowly come back to full awareness of your surroundings.

15. Log the information in a journal and note the limiting beliefs that play a significant role in your fears. Continue honing and rewriting your beliefs until it feels natural and you experience the cha-ching effect.

16. Wait a day and repeat the exercise with your new tribal belief.

A FEW IMPORTANT POINTS TO REMEMBER

- Don't get discouraged. The first few times you may have difficulty calming the pond's surface. Stay with it, and it will get much easier.
- You may need to repeat this exercise several times before you allow yourself to see your Truth. Do not give up; it will come.
- Once you uncover the actual reason for your discomfort, rewrite your limiting belief in increments as described earlier in the book.
- It may take several visits to the pond to come to peace with your decision.
- Be gentle with yourself during this process. Your patience will be rewarded with a powerful outcome.

Facing your fears head-on may seem like an insurmountable task at this moment. The paradox is that facing your fears will actually make you feel safer. The unknown is scary, because you don't know how to deal with it. Do you remember the *Star Wars* movie when Yoda sent Luke Skywalker into the cave to battle

his demons? Luke imagined all kinds of horrors in that cave—
he was terrified. Yet the reality was there was nothing but darkness in that cave—no scary monsters—just Luke's imagination
that caused fear. You and Luke share that common foe.

Don't let your imagination get the better of you. Use it for greater things.

If you are willing to explore your fear and continue the pond
exercise, some amazing things will happen.

- Your body will begin to desensitize to rote responses
  to fear: your stomach won't get tight, your back won't
  hurt, and your mind won't go "off-line."
- When faced with a new or difficult decision, you will
  be able think more clearly, and your automatic response will not be "I can't do that," but rather, "Perhaps it's possible."
- It will be easier to rewrite those limiting beliefs
  that once seemed insurmountable and too tough to
  tackle—because now you know the true reason for
  your loyalty: being worried about your reputation because of an unhealthy third chakra (refer to the section
  "Healing Your Resentment" for ways to begin healing).
- The mental Ping-Pong disappears.
- You will begin to feel safe enough to be in your body.
- You will learn to welcome guidance. (Speaking of
  guidance, not feeling safe in the world is exaggerated
  when you are also afraid of God's judgment about

you. If this is the case for you, be sure you take plenty of time looking at your tribal beliefs about God.)

- The greatest result you will experience is that the logistical concerns associated with your decision that once overwhelmed and frightened you will become easier to handle, and at times dissolve away.

A natural progression occurs on the energetic plane when you make a decision in alignment with your spirit. You send out an energetic broadcast that says you are ready for a synchronistic experience. You will experience both synchrodivinity (everything you need to know is there for you, if you take the time to listen), and synchronicity (when a coincidence, a sign, a chance encounter, or an unexpected experience confirms what you already know).

I have seen people joyously and easily leave corporate life, end their professional practices, start businesses, get married, get divorced, sell their houses, and go on longed-for trips, a short time after they claimed it would be near impossible to do so.

You might think from what I've written that everyone who has safety issues or tribal beliefs that make them feel unsafe will suffer from anxiety or come down with colds, flu, skin ailments, or an autoimmune disease. This is absolutely not true. The key factor is the amount of conflict someone is in. If someone is completely disconnected from his or her soul, that person can follow all the toxic tribal beliefs in the world and not fall ill. But if your intention is to wake up spiritually, having tribal beliefs about the world not being a safe place will cause tremendous conflict with your soul.

The wear and tear on the body from such conflict is immense. It is no wonder the human body can age prematurely when someone lives with chronic fear. I have seen people who are as much as thirty energetic years older than their physical age. Yet this all changes when you examine and change your deeply held tribal beliefs. I cannot begin to recount the amount of healing and freedom I have seen people gain from simply being willing to change a tribal belief.

Renee came to me with a puzzling case of exercised-induced asthma that had lasted almost twenty years. It particularly interfered with her life because her love was exercise, and she was a popular and sought-after personal trainer. My Reading of Renee revealed that she was in a chronic state of mild fight-or-flight all the time. I saw that at age six she had experienced an event that changed her life forever. When I asked Renee what she remembered from back then, she replied, "That was when my sister was born. When they brought her home from the hospital, it felt like my mother ignored me completely from that time on. I felt orphaned, abandoned, I was treated differently."

As a result, Renee had developed the tribal belief *The world is not a safe place.* Unfortunately, that tribal belief now got triggered every time she thought she was ignored or misunderstood. Because Renee's marriage was marked by episodes of feeling ignored (abandoned) and her subsequent feelings of mild panic, it was as if she was in a constant mild panic attack all the time.

Then, whenever Renee's mild panic grew, it would ignite a feeling of suffocation that eventually translated into a physical reality.

I helped Renee rewrite her tribal belief to *It's reasonable to believe that it's possible to feel safety in the world at times.* We had to go gently because after so many years of believing a certain way, her energy system would not have accepted a tribal belief that was the complete opposite of the one she had held on to for so very long.

The last I heard, Renee's asthma had greatly subsided. Her marriage was slowly improving, too. She had changed her old energetic broadcast to her husband that it was okay to abandon her. It was still difficult for him to be authentic with her, but Renee felt much less triggered by her husband's actions. When she felt more safe, she took a few risks and found that people were receptive to her Healing Touch work. This began to be an enormous source of connection and authenticity for Renee as she explored her capacity for channeling healing energy. She was no longer suffocating from her tribal belief that the world was not a safe place to be.

Remember, the wording on your particular tribal beliefs may vary slightly, but the energetic message is the same: there is no real safety; you must be good, work hard, hide your feelings, and behave according to the rules to be safe; and you cannot take risks because should you fail, mistakes will be punished.

SOME QUESTIONS TO HELP YOU UNCOVER YOUR TRIBAL BELIEFS

1. Have you ever worried about becoming a bag lady?
2. Do you find the need to control inconsequential things in your life?

3. Is it hard for you to relax?

4. Do you celebrate your achievements?

TRIBAL BELIEFS ABOUT BEING SAFE IN THE WORLD

1. The world is not a safe place.
2. If you are not vigilant in life, things will go to hell in a handbasket.
3. It's not safe to get too close to people. You risk rejection and that's not survivable.
4. If things are too good, they're going to get taken away.
5. I'm always waiting for the worst to happen.
6. There is always a price to pay for sins.
7. It's not safe to be happy.
8. Something bad is going to happen; bad things always happen.
9. If I'm good, I will be safe.
10. The only way to get to heaven is not to sin.
11. I can never do anything right.
12. The more you have, the safer you are.
13. Don't get too relaxed, because something's going to happen.
14. Play it safe, you never know what will happen.
15. Save for a rainy day, but if it rains try not to use the money. You might need it later.

You have learned many valuable and important things. Here are just a few of them:

- A technique to conquer some of your fears.
- How to identify a conflict within you.
- How to rewrite a limiting belief.
- What conflict does to your body, mind, and spirit.
- Your judgments and criticisms are based on limiting beliefs.
- The voice of your spirit is guidance and will always lead you to a better place.

But let's not stop here. You've done some great work exploring your unconscious and limiting beliefs. You've been courageous and rewrote some of them. You've been willing to face the root of some of your fears, and you are ready to reap the rewards of your efforts. Now it's time to make a commitment to live at the highest vibration possible and share that healing energy with the world.

10.

The Excitement of Living Vibrationally

LISTENING TO YOUR SPIRIT RESULTS IN

WONDROUS POSSIBILITIES

D o you remember the Beach Boys singing, "Good, good, good, good vibrations"? Let's make that your motto. Remember that I want you to be wildly happy, incredibly successful, and filled with passion and spontaneity. Listening to your spirit will accomplish all of it. And when your vibrations are good, you are sending out the best possible energy to the rest of the world. The fact is, your good vibrations are healing to others. You can access the healer within you by answering a few simple questions:

1. Are you living at the highest vibration possible?
2. Are you living your truth or your tribe's?
3. Is your life authentic, or do you do many things because you believe you have to?
4. Do your relationships, way of life, type of exercise, activities, or profession raise or lower your vibration?

When you listen to your spirit, you will hear what is good for you. When you try to live the life that others want for you, there's a good chance it will not be in your highest good.

Let's talk about your friend of ten years. Lately you've noticed it's a bit of a drain to spend time with him; it's not fun or vitalizing to be together. To begin, ask yourself: Does this friendship raise or lower my vibration? There will be no discussion, debate, or maybes. The answer is simply yes or no. Look at how you feel after spending time with your friend. Next, look at your tribal beliefs about friendship. Many people believe *A friend of long standing is a friend for life.* This tribal belief will stand in the way of you doing what's good for you. Logically you understand that often people grow apart, but the tribal belief is firm. You must stay friends. So you continue to drain your energy by making excuses to not see him and then feeling badly. This waffling can go on for years—or minutes. It's your choice.

Go back to the simple question:

- Does this relationship raise or lower your vibration? If you sit quietly and set an intention to hear your Truth, you will.

Next identify why it lowers your vibration.

- Does he complain all the time but has no real desire to improve his life? Is he sarcastic or cynical all the time? Do you share no common interests?

Be truthful and there is room to grow. For example, if his cynicism gets you down, mention it. He has the choice to change or not. Often people are not conscious of how they are acting. You may salvage a friendship. But if the two of you simply don't click anymore, it will be major work to keep the relationship going. And it will be strained, inauthentic, and dreadful.

Finally, ask yourself if your tribal belief about long-standing friends is in your highest good.

- Does this tribal belief raise or lower your vibration? By this point, you already know the answer. It's time to rewrite that belief and set yourself free from a friendship that no longer interests or excites you.

It takes tremendous work to ignore the voice of your soul, the energy of God within you—that is, until eventually you become so disconnected from your spirit that you can do it unconsciously. Tribal beliefs that lower your vibration cause you to disconnect from your spirit. That's how you are able to maintain them. If you disconnect from your spirit, you can continue to exist, but who wants mere existence? I want to live an authentic, passionate, and dynamic life that includes exciting thoughts, inspiration, and the ability to discern and trust my intuition. I'd bet anything that you do, too.

When you heal your spirit and reconnect with the part of you most like God, I guarantee that amazing changes will begin in your life. I see this every time people make the decision to live vibrationally. I see people able to honestly evaluate situations rather than get into a heavy analysis about the ins and outs of their dilemma. If a situation raises your vibration, you know it. If it doesn't, you'll either say, "Well, I don't really know . . . Parts of it do, parts of it don't . . ." or you'll try to talk yourself into how much it does raise your vibration. I'm here to tell you, it either does or it doesn't. There is no middle ground in this one. It's like being pregnant. Either you are or you're not. There's no "sort of" being pregnant!

So you see, living vibrationally is quite simple. Whatever you are doing, eating, or saying either raises your vibration—which causes you to feel happy, excited, and passionate—or it doesn't. Living vibrationally makes life's choices simple and direct. There is nothing to debate. Your choices either lead you toward true joy and empowerment or they do not.

Sometimes, the questions you must ask yourself are difficult. For example, examining your current relationships—including friends *and* mates—can bring you answers you might not want to hear. But the fact remains that whatever the situation, the question you need to ask is simple: "Does this relationship raise or lower my vibration?" Living this way requires you to be honest with yourself. If you don't want to know the truth, you will feel unsure and answer "I don't know."

When that happens I have a solution for you. Flip a coin with the promise that you will do what it says: "Heads I stay in the relationship, tails I leave." Long before the coin drops into your hands, you will know the answer. Many times I have flipped a coin for a client and just as it reaches my hand, he or she shouts, "Don't let it be heads!" On other occasions, before I even reveal how the coin has landed, the person knows the answer.

Trust me when I say, if something raises your vibration, you will know it. If you think you are not sure, it's because you are afraid to admit that your vibration is lowered by a particular person, activity, or way of life.

It takes great courage to start living vibrationally because it will require you to be rigorously honest about where you are putting your energy in life. And before you start thinking that I am condoning a self-centered way of life, consider this: How self-centered do you think you become when you are resentful, angry, and conflicted because you are doing something you don't want to? Quite a lot.

Living vibrationally doesn't mean avoiding the things you dislike—it means living in integrity with your spirit.

When you live vibrationally, you can take responsibility for your happiness. If you feel trapped, find and change the tribal belief that is trapping you. If you feel resentful, look at the situation you have chosen in order to remain true to your tribe. And if you are unhappy, look around you and see the people your tribe insists you keep in your life.

I must say a word of warning about this last suggestion. I have met many women and a few men in what are clearly difficult, sometimes abusive, or extremely negative relationships and who think that they are doing something spiritually wonderful by staying in a situation that is clearly eroding their soul. This is an example of the tribal belief *Spiritual growth is hard, and you have to change yourself so you can be happy in any situation with any person at all times.* Personally, I don't believe this at all. It is responsible for more people staying in bad situations than any other tribal belief about spirituality.

It's up to you to decide how high (or low) a vibration you are willing to live at. You should know, however, that you are capable of a much higher vibration than your current one. My job is to help you find out where you are hemorrhaging precious energy and teach you how to stop, if you so desire. I hope it is becoming clearer to you how much energy you lose when you try to follow your tribal beliefs instead of your spirit—and how easy it is to fix those energy leaks. That is, unless you subscribe to the belief *Personal growth is hard work, serious work. It requires intense devotion and at the end, all you find is that you need more of it.*

Choosing to live vibrationally will affect your life in big and small ways, yet some people get confused and think that to live vibrationally, they must first be quite spiritual. They've got it backward. When you ignore trying to be spiritual and focus on living at a high vibration (which means you are happy, healthy, and passionate), you are in touch with your spirit. Hence, you already *are* being spiritual: you are living according to your guidance and intuition. Being spiritual simply means you have learned to listen to your soul, a skill that always raises your vibration.

During one of my workshops, I asked people what they did to enhance their spiritual growth. Then I sat back, excited to hear about their joys and passions. Their answers, however, ranged from astounding to absurd. Muriel forced herself to recite positive affirmations at her altar each morning, even though this routine often made her late for work and invited the ire of her boss. Gracie performed a cleansing ritual each evening, even though she admitted that after a grueling day what she really wanted was to go out for an ice cream sundae. Sarah awoke each morning at five to meditate no matter what. She was very disciplined—and very stiff at the end of her thirty minutes. One of my favorite moments in that workshop occurred when she burst out with excitement, "I don't even *like* meditation! And I hate getting up so early!" She made the room laugh so hard, it raised all our vibrations!

A few weeks later Sarah told us she had begun meditating occasionally, for much shorter periods, and was enjoying it immensely. (In other words, it was raising her vibration.) This was the difference between Sarah meditating according to a tribal belief—*If you meditate regularly for long periods of time, you will achieve enlightenment*—versus meditating according to her vibration. When Sarah had the whole room laughing, she looked much more enlightened than when she was trying to force herself to be spiritual by following a prescribed path. The peace and joy that emanated from her weeks later told us all that meditating according to her vibration was really working for her.

In another workshop, I worked intensely with a woman who was battling many tribal beliefs about work, being productive, and being an upstanding, taxpaying citizen. The problem was, Jessie was battling a recurrence of cancer and needed to take time off from work. Her energetic blueprint was clear *(Take a rest!)* and so were her tribal beliefs *(Keep working and be productive or else you are lazy)*. Jessie finally agreed to consider taking "a healing sabbatical." The idea of going on disability was overwhelming for her because she felt strong enough to continue working. Eventually, however, she considered taking a period of time off that had a specific purpose (in her case, to heal).

The turning point came when I asked her if there was something she would really love to do. "Go to Hawaii for two weeks," she promptly replied. Not only did Jessie go on a healing sabbatical, she spent two weeks basking in the tropical beauty of the Hawaiian Islands. On her return, she was radiant. The good feelings from her Hawaiian adventure inspired her to travel more, and she arranged to visit friends all over the United States. She made her trips relaxing, full of rest and fun. Jessie enjoyed herself more than she ever had in her life, and she even gave herself permission to buy herself her dream car: a red convertible. She called me on her way home from the dealership, deliriously happy as she raced up the California coastline.

Eventually the cancer returned and overtook her, but not before she became happy and at peace. Jessie had learned to live vibrationally, and the last year of her life was the happiest she ever had. Her death saddened me, but it did not surprise me. (It is not everyone's desire to heal physically from illness, despite their words to the contrary.) But how much better it was for Jessie to spend what time she had left being happy rather than being productive at her corporate job. Jessie successfully changed her tribal belief to *There are many ways to be productive, and being happy is one of them.*

Living vibrationally can bring happiness to your life in small ways, too. Marylou wanted to spend the week before the New Year by herself. She envisioned a wonderful hermitlike week filled with reflection, prayer, and solitude. She knew it was exactly what she needed. First her friends hated her choice, demanding she spend the time off with them. Next her family questioned her choice, judging it to be a form of depression about the new year. Third, her boyfriend was hurt that she would choose a destination and experience that excluded him.

Marylou relented and compromised to the hilt. She agreed to spend half the week with her friends, family, and boyfriend, and the last three days on her own. By the end of the first three days, she felt so conflicted and resentful doing what she didn't want to, she was worn out and chose to stay home after all. Her concern for everyone's feelings and their judgments about her had left her feeling exhausted and deflated.

Marylou's spirit wanted solitude, but her tribe demanded her presence. By compromising herself, she experienced a severe energy drain. The little energy she had left was used to convince herself that her need for solitude wasn't that important. The conflict with her soul created duress, resentment, exhaustion, and apathy for the first three days of the holiday week. In other words, she was disconnected from what she was feeling, doing, and saying and had a lousy time. And all because of her tribal beliefs about what it meant to be a good daughter, sister, friend, and girlfriend. Fortunately, Marylou was not married or her conflict would have included the guilt about not being a good wife and mother.

Alexis, who was recovering from cancer, believed *You should be nice to people all the time, even if they are crappy to you.* A naturally plucky woman, Alexis often had to swallow her reactions and stifle any colorful retorts. It took a lot of energy to force herself to do something that always made her feel so drained and was so against her true nature. It wasn't until she came to a workshop that she realized how damaging her lack of action was becoming to her.

She told the group how a friend frequently called her and offered the unsolicited advice that because Alexis had cancer, it was essential to eat a lot of broccoli. Now, Alexis hates broccoli, but she was nice to the woman each time she called. As she relayed this information to us, she suddenly started to laugh. "I hate broccoli," she sputtered between waves of laughter. "And I can't stand it when people tell me what I need to do in order to heal—especially when I haven't asked for their advice! I've been suffering through her phone calls when I could have been eating chocolate and taking a hot bath. I can't believe I have been so loyal to a belief that isn't *me*. I don't even agree with it." Alexis set herself free by changing her belief that afternoon. She felt wonderful. That night when her friend called and launched into the broccoli lecture, Alexis told her how she really felt about broccoli and unsolicited advice. And then she went out for a hot fudge sundae. The amount that she raised her vibration by speaking her truth did her health far more good than eating a ton of broccoli!

Raising your vibration doesn't just affect your life, it will also affect the lives of others. I've talked about the ripple effect—you know we are all connected and I know, like Tracy, you want to do something positive in this world—perhaps even be of service to others. Raising your vibration allows you to do this without exhausting yourself.

Before Tracy fell on hard financial times, she supported various charitable organizations like the Red Cross. She helped people out of work, unwed mothers, and children with no hope for college. She was a wonderful humanitarian. Yet, when Tracy lost her own job, her efforts ceased. Because she would not accept any financial help—not unemployment checks, not assistance from her family, and eventually not welfare, she could no longer be of service to others. The reason? Her tribal beliefs:

- Charity is for people who truly need it.
- Charity is for people who can't find a job.
- People who take money/charity when they don't really need it are thieves and the lowest form of human beings.

Look at the impact on herself and others because of her limiting beliefs:

- They ended her humanitarian efforts.
- They caused worry for her friends and family.
- They stressed her immune system as survival became an issue that caused her to feel unsafe.
- Tracy felt doubly conflicted: first, because she wouldn't accept charity and was scared and, second, because she could not be of service.

There is no doubt that Tracy suffered because of her limiting beliefs. When she rewrote her beliefs, she gained much more than simply financial help during crisis. She learned what it felt like to be on the receiving end of charity, making her a more compassionate and empathetic humanitarian. She understands more clearly the pride that prevents people from seeking help, and the shame that sometimes follows. Now when she talks to those in need, her authenticity shines through and helps ease the hearts and minds of those in need.

Once you do something because some tribal belief says you are supposed to or because you think you should (thanks to an unconscious tribal belief), resentment can easily build. When you consciously choose what you do, you have the choice to allow your vibration to be lowered or raised. If there are people you don't like, move away from them. If someone is boring you to tears, go to the bathroom. Take charge of your vibration, enjoy your newfound freedom, and bring some laughter and goodness to the event.

To engage on a path of higher learning, spiritual evolution, creativity—whatever your calling—you need inspiration. The very nature of inspiration demands you to be open to new possibilities. What if Picasso had not dared to think outside of his tribe and try a new technique? Would we have Beethoven's music now had he not dared to play what was considered discordant and awful music in the early nineteenth century? These individuals had the courage to look beyond their tribes and listen to their spirits.

MIRACLES

As C. S. Lewis wrote, "We are often unaware of the most significant moments of our lives." (Perhaps this is why people believe that miracles are so rare.)

Once you have such an epiphany, it is almost impossible to avoid a sacred choice in favor of what you know, deep down from the roots of your soul, is true. It doesn't matter if your tribes laugh at you. Follow your intuition and take a risk. Summon the courage to make something else more important than your fear of being ostracized and laughed at. Became a hero—someone who makes a journey to show the rest of us that we, too, can make that journey.

People are skeptical when I tell them this process really works, that you can change the beliefs of a lifetime this easily. If you are one of these skeptics, I recommend exploring the tribal belief that says change has to be long and hard.

So what are you waiting for? Isn't it time to seek out your Truth and live at a good vibration? You know the benefits for yourself and others. Today can be the day you make a sacred choice and begin to live your life in integrity with your spirit—the part of you that is of the highest vibration. Today can be the day you stop wasting valuable time trying to be who you are not—leaving plenty of time to nurture yourself, take care of others, and be of service.

Do you remember how to recognize a limiting tribal belief that is causing you conflict?

1. **Notice the emotional warning signs of a limiting tribal belief:**
   - Feeling frustrated or trapped like you have no choices.
   - Feeling resentful that you have to do something.
   - Feeling tired from playing mental Ping-Pong between what you want to do versus what you are supposed to do.
   - Feeling guilty.
2. **Be willing to admit your spirit is in conflict with your tribe.**
3. **Put into words exactly what you think you should be doing.**
4. **Explain why you should be doing it.** The "why" will give you a good idea of what your tribal belief is. Try to find the exact right words to express it: when you write or speak the limiting belief, it may exacerbate the feelings above.

5. **Ask yourself, if there were no logistical considerations, what you would *really* want to do.** The answer to this question gets you past all your excuses: if no one was hurt by your actions, no one became angry at you, and everyone supported your decision, what would you do? This is where your spirit gets a voice.

6. **Does your answer energize or drain you?** Sit in a quiet place and talk to your spirit—not your mind—and I promise you will get a very clear answer. Ask yourself, does it raise or lower your vibrations? Does it make you happier? Does it contribute to your spiritual evolution or slow it down? The answer is either yes or no. There are no mental gymnastics involved. Either the answer does or it does not. If your answer does not energize you, excite you, or raise you up, then you are still operating under a limiting tribal belief. This is an important choice point for you.

II.

Being an Inspiration to Others

WHAT TRIBAL BELIEFS ARE YOU GOING TO
PASS ON TO THE NEXT GENERATION?

Tribal beliefs severely slow or limit your spiritual evolution. If you are not on a spiritual path or aren't interested in your purpose in life, then carry on as usual. You will evolve spiritually at the rate of your tribe. If you have ever tried to coordinate fourteen family members in picking a restaurant and meeting there at the same time for dinner, then you understand how a tribe operates and can imagine just how fast it evolves. Or worse, have you ever been to Disneyland and been stuck behind a slow and distracted, apathetic person? You are excited and ready to explode with joy—you can't wait to get to Space Mountain—yet you are stuck behind a man who is ambling along, because he doesn't want to be at the park. One look at his family trailing behind and his ripple effect is obvious. It feels stifling and you can't wait to move around him. That's how it feels when you come across a tribal belief that's been standing in the way of your health or happiness. Once you have identified and rewritten your limiting beliefs, you will have cleared a huge hurdle in your spiritual path. And your life will change for the better immediately.

People usually underestimate the power of tribal beliefs—wars are waged for them, terrible suffering is endured for them, and a stagnant existence is the reward for following them. I've given you many, many reasons for changing those inherited beliefs. Here's one more: do it for the common good!

Even though it may feel frightening, thinking outside of your tribe just might be the best gift you ever give them. Consider a simple act like creating fire. If someone had not thought outside the way of the tribe way back when, we wouldn't have matches now. Tribes that are weighed down by old, old beliefs cannot adapt to new circumstances. They need your new ideas, even your new leadership. Each time you are true to your spirit, you are presenting the tribe with a new role model. Your actions may anger or annoy some members of the tribe, but they may also inspire other members to change.

HERO

*A person who takes a journey to inspire others
to find their own courage.*

Shelley decided not to attend a family Thanksgiving dinner because a cousin Shelley really disliked had been invited. Shelley had expressly asked her mother not to invite this cousin. Lorene always drank too much and was disliked by the rest of the family as well. A dreadful fight ensued because of Shelley's decision. Her parents were especially critical. However, a year later, her mother came to Shelley and said, "You know, it never occurred to me that I had a choice about Lorene. But in the last few months, I haven't gone to occasions where she's been invited, and I feel so much better! I'm sorry for the things I said to you, and I'm sorry I didn't support your decision."

Do you see what happened? There was an initial kerfuffle—that's a ruckus—because someone dared to speak her truth. However, it had an extremely positive ripple effect. Within a couple of years the entire tribe had changed. They began to get together without the negative influence of a practicing alcoholic. It made family gatherings more peaceful and taught the children that you do not have to let yourself be around unpleasantness just because someone is family.

As you evolve spiritually, you will more easily recognize the limiting beliefs that are not in alignment with your highest potential.

As every visionary knows, when you reject the status quo and start thinking for yourself, you become a tribe of one. This doesn't last long, though. Before you know it, others are looking at you as a role model and making wonderful changes in their lives, too. Suddenly your new way of thinking—and the happiness you are experiencing—has spread.

We talked earlier about the old tribal belief *No pain, no gain.* Why would you pass on this belief to new members of your tribe? If you happen to be in a gym, *No pain, no gain* means that you must work out until it hurts. That's how people injure themselves! Do you really want to model this behavior to your children?

Now imagine applying the principle of *No pain, no gain* to money or happiness. What if you're really good at business and you make money easily? Then there are the people who either give their money away to ungrateful family members (after all, *Family helps family* and *You have so much, you should help your family out*) or lost great sums through bad investments because they had a tribal belief that said *It's not okay to have money (or happiness!) when your family doesn't.* Why would anyone who knew better want to pass this belief on?

I have watched countless people buy homes because it is a

tribal belief in American culture that it's the American dream—and nowadays the only way to secure your financial future. Now, owning your own home can be wonderful, but what if in order to obey that tribal belief, you strap yourself financially, end up living in a neighborhood or home you don't like because it's all you can afford, work overtime to pay your mortgage when your heart wants to see the world or spend time with your kids, and/or get trapped in a job you don't like in order to make that big payment? It's not the act of buying a home that is good or bad, it's the motivation for your decision. Are you blindly following a tribal belief or are you choosing to do something that raises your vibration? Are you being a follower or a tribal leader?

One woman I know bought a house without realizing there was an alternative. The market was heating up, she was engaged to be married, it was the thing to do. Had she thought about it (as she did years later), Vivian would have realized she didn't want the responsibility of maintaining a yard or hiring a gardener, she didn't want to be involved in decorating a home, she didn't want all that space, and she didn't like the suburbs. She took the time to listen to her spirit and found her truth: the house felt like a noose around her neck. She sold her house, shocking her family and neighbors, and found the ultimate living place in a chic downtown condo.

Her newfound freedom and happiness was contagious. Her sister, Beth, called her, saying, "If you can sell your house, so can I!" Beth was delighted to live in a maintenance-free condo, admitting she, too, hated the burden of being a homeowner but had been afraid to sell her home.

Being an inspiration doesn't always require big measures like selling your home. It can be as simple as:

1. Choosing one day to volunteer and serve meals in a soup kitchen. You'll feel great, and your high vibration and happiness will caress those you love.

2. Choosing to find humor in a difficult situations, rather than complaining. There is a contagious and healing aspect to laughter.

3. Deciding to lose some weight. It's always easier when you have a friend to stand by you, and you'll be a great motivator for a friend.

4. Instead of saying, "I cannot," try saying, "I can." Choose to do something that inspires you like raising money for a good cause by walking for multiple sclerosis or breast cancer, hiking the Grand Canyon for leukemia, or bicycling for ALS. When your family and friends find out, they may decide to join you. Be the person who takes the first step.

5. Sometimes it's as simple as speaking up among friends—it gives them the courage to do the same. I know a women's group who has a great time at events, except for when one cantankerous woman participates. Finally one of the women spoke up and said she didn't enjoy the complaining, arguing, and all-around low vibration. She spoke up and ended the problem.

Today is a great day to raise your vibration and let it ripple out into the world. What a great gift to give others.

In Chapter 1, I introduced you to Debra, who thought *A woman shouldn't outshine her husband.* Taught by her mother that a smart, witty girl would never find a husband, Debra was afraid she would be alone for the rest of her life. Hiding her true nature, especially in the face of her husband's resentment for her success at work, had taken a toll upon Debra's health. Her thyroid became dysfunctional and she was often tired.

One day while resting on the couch, Debra's moment of truth arrived, and she cleanly rose to the occasion. She realized that being alone was far better than having no life at all, which is exactly what profound fatigue was doing to her. She decided to take back her spirit by rewriting her tribal belief.

When Debra told me of her sacred choice, I encouraged her to explore her talents and gifts and own them. This brought up another tribal belief of hers: *It's not okay to blow your own horn.* I reminded Debra that our talents are gifts from God or a Higher Power, and when you don't acknowledge a gift it is a form of snubbing. I explained that recognizing my own gifts and talents is my way of being grateful and saying thank you to God. Whether you have a smart brain; are creative, compassionate, and a good listener; or are athletic, if you don't acknowledge your gifts, you'll never be able to fully use them. In fact, if God calls you to be of service by using your gifts and talents, you won't be able rise to the occasion since you won't know—or admit—you have any!

Two weeks later, I found a happy, energetic, and talented woman excited by the possibilities in her new life. After she rewrote her tribal belief to *It is reasonable to believe that a good woman shines her brightest in all situations—it is a way of thanking God for her talents and gifts,* Debra was asked to join the board of the local library. Having a lifetime interest in reading, she was delighted. This was a wonderful match for her interests and talents. She quickly found a wonderful calling and was recognized for her diligent work for the library. Her peak moment came when she was publicly recognized for her community efforts. She looked radiant from the podium!

Now, what do you suppose Debra's story taught other people in her life, especially young women? That it is their duty to suppress their brains and talent so as not to make the men in their lives feel bad? Or that if their idea of happiness was to become a research scientist, an astronaut, an opera star, or a wildly successful CEO, they should go for it? And what do you think is a more useful tribal belief to pass on to the young people around you? This: *Don't admit you have any talents or gifts.* Or this: *Acknowledging your talents and gifts so you can enjoy using them is a way of being grateful!*

I know a wonderful man in his seventies who is about to turn eighteen. One of his dreams is to bodysurf at dawn in the warm waters of Australia. Naturally, he has many obligations and things that stood in the way of his dream. In a workshop I noted how high his vibration was when talking about bodysurfing, and asked him, "Why aren't you doing it?"

This was an important moment: he could rationalize all the reasons he couldn't go to Australia or he could search for his truth. After all, he had many commitments to his wife, family, and work; his life was busy. He had limiting beliefs about work *(Working is the sign of a good man)* and about being a good husband *(A good husband thinks of himself last)* that conflicted with his desire to goof off and have fun in the surf.

He made a profound decision to listen to the yearnings of his spirit and rewrite some limiting beliefs. He changed his schedule, told his wife about his dream, and an amazing thing happened: his wife burst into the biggest, most beautiful smile I've ever seen. She morphed into a playful and excited teenager because her husband had chosen to honor himself.

They went to Australia and bodysurfed and realized they liked having more free time together. They decided to keep a lighter schedule and live a less planned and more spontaneous life. His decisive moment changed both their lives. They became more aware of some choices they made that were based on limiting beliefs. Their new choices are based on taking care of themselves and being happy.

They chose to lead their own lives, be true to their spirits, and live at a high vibration. What an incredible gift they have given each other. They are an inspiration to others because of their choices.

Rewriting just one limiting belief can dramatically change and enhance your life and be the incentive for someone you care about.

Epilogue:
Slay Your Dragons

Madison didn't know she was ready for her journey when she came to me with a series of gynecological problems. A history of surgeries had taken their toll and she feared her health was rapidly deteriorating. A tribal belief that she owed her son everything to help him be successful and that a good mother devotes herself completely to the happiness of her child was in conflict with her guidance. Unfortunately, Madison's twenty-five-year-old son was not as interested in his success as his mother was. He was much more interested in drinking, video games, and, in general, getting away with doing as little as possible.

Madison is an interesting woman in a physically demanding job. Years of smoking had given her a husky, almost sultry voice. Although she had been tromped on by men and by life, taught that she was powerless, worthless, and unlovable, there was not an iota of victim energy or a smidgen of self-pity in her. In fact, this woman is a hero.

I watched a miracle unfold when I Read her energetic blueprint. It was one of those divine moments of synchrodivinity that so often come with little fanfare but huge results. She stared at me intently, nodded slightly, and straightened up as she heard the voice of her spirit for the first time. All of the negativity she had learned as a child began to dissolve as she made a sacred choice to listen to that new voice. Madison wrote down my instructions for changing a tribal belief and started writing a new one, unaware of the miracle that had just occurred.

When I saw her a month later, the transformation was delightful and profound. Madison's face had softened and she radiated with the glow of someone who has discovered her self-confidence. When I asked her about her son, she solidly replied, "It's not my journey; if I spend time where I don't belong, I won't have the energy to be where God needs me." Her energy was clean, clear, and definite. She felt her new resolve tested when her son was in a minor car accident. She declined to get involved, knowing that she did not belong in straightening out his messes. She had rewritten her tribal to *A good mother takes care of herself first and teaches her grown children to take responsibility for them-*

selves. Her energy was much higher and her health problems were resolving.

> ## COURAGE
>
> *Momentarily allowing one thing—a thought, action, desire—to be more important than your fear.*

Madison's willingness stirs me; she dared to take the hero's journey—the journey that others are afraid to take. Her courage, tenacity, and desire to have something more than what she has known have driven her to more happiness and a brighter future than she thought was possible. It is the Madisons of the world who show each of us what is possible when we decide that something else is more important than keeping our beliefs unchanged.

I salute Madison, who chose to slay her dragons and is an inspiration to so many people wanting a better life. In the spirit of the hero, I ask you to take a journey of your own. Pay attention to your tribals and examine your reaction to them. Are they right for you? Do they raise your vibration and make you happy? Are they in alignment with your spirit, or are they simply dragons that it is time for you to slay?

Is there a hero within you? When your tribe tells you that you can only make money by working extremely hard, yet somewhere deep inside of you, there is a spiritual whisper that says, *That's just not true,* you are on the brink of an extraordinary moment, a moment offering you a sacred choice. Will you listen to the whispering of your soul? Will you follow in the footsteps of courageous men and women through the centuries and consider a new possibility for your life?

Say yes, and in one incredible moment your spirit will be heard and your spiritual evolution will begin. I celebrate you as you listen to your inspiration and become a hero in your own life and in the lives of others. You are joining an amazing new tribe—the tribe of people who listen to their spirits—and your life will become dramatically easier and happier.

A sacred choice is an extremely personal decision for each of us. Only you can make that decision. By listening to your spirit, by having a good relationship with God—it's amazing how much easier this is once you change those tribal beliefs about who God is and what God thinks of you—and by being willing to heal yourself, the choice will be clear. And thanks to the ripple effect, everyone around you will feel your happiness and high vibration. What a wonderful gift to give the world.

I am excited by the enlightened tribal beliefs you will pass on to the next generation!

Index

ABOUT THE AUTHOR

CHRISTEL NANI, RN, is a profoundly gifted clairvoyant with a background in emergency medicine. Her ability to Read complete strangers—and in a few moments know them better than they know themselves—has ignited her reputation as the real thing. Author of *Diary of a Medical Intuitive* and *Guidance 24/7,* Christel is inspired by people who refuse to be victims—most especially Tina Turner.

A natural spiritual teacher, her vision for the future is simple: "To teach enough people to live at their highest vibration, which will ripple out into the world, creating *the tipping point toward positivity.*"

To learn more about her work, visit her at www.ChristelNani.com.